The Micah Mandate is a message fitly spoken for our times. Amid the many voices clamoring for an audience, there are few who speak with prophetic urgency. George Grant writes from a deep reservoir of study, prayer and discipleship. Those who take the time to listen will hear God's clear call to justice, mercy and humility.

Steve Green
Recording Artist

THE MICAH MANDATE

"What does the Lord
require of you?
To act justly and
to love mercy and
to walk humbly
with your God."

Micah 6:8

GEORGE GRANT

MOODY PRESS
CHICAGO

To Stephen Mansfield and Tom Clark
Epitomes of the Mandate

and

To Billy Amos and Steven Wilkins
Evidences of the Mandate

CONTENTS

ACKNOWLEDGMENTS

*The greatest part of a writer's time is spent
in reading, in order to write: a man will
turn over half a library to make one book.*
Samuel Johnson

*Those who are in rebellion against memory
are the ones who wish to live without knowledge.*
Richard Weaver

"The only possible excuse for this book," G. K. Chesterton once wrote in a preface, "is that it is an answer to a challenge. Even a bad shot is dignified when he accepts a duel."[1]
Though written nearly a century ago, Chesterton's remark describes my justification for this project. It grew out of a challenge. That challenge came from many of my dearest and most trusted friends. Together they encouraged me to put into words and into print the thoughts and reflections that have shaped my inner and outer walks over the past twenty years. I can only pray that this "bad shot" may indeed be "dignified" by rising to the occasion.

In his case, Chesterton quipped that such a challenge "was perhaps an incautious suggestion to make to a person only too ready to write books upon the feeblest provocation."[2]

Again, his description fits my own case. Even so, it was only the support and encouragement of those stalwart friends that enabled me to actually *work out* what has taken so long to *work in*.

Jim Bell, Greg Thornton, Cheryl Dunlop, Bill Thrasher, and Linda Holland at Moody Press believed in this project even when it was little more than a fuzzy notion and a sketchy outline—and even when it was frighteningly overdue. My pastors—Jim

Bachmann and Ian Sears—and my circle of confidants and men-
tors—my dad, Howard Phillips, Robert Dotson, Rus Walton,
David Dunham, D. James Kennedy, Stephen Mansfield, David
Vaughan, Tom Clark, Lane Adams, and Charles Wolfe—inspired
me by their lives of balance and reinforced the notion that biblical
balance can indeed be lived out in very practical ways. Gene and
Susan Hunt and the other members of the PCA Christian
Education and Publications Study Tour tolerated my preoccupa-
tion with this book while I was supposed to be showing them the
sights. Much of the manuscript was initially outlined in snatches
while we were together in Israel and Holland. That they still happily followed me hither and yon is no less evidence of their long-
suffering than of God's grace. My former coworkers at Coral Ridge
Ministries, the Christian Worldview Institute, and Legacy
Communications stood by me through thick and thin—even when
there was a lot less thick than thin. And my students at the
Franklin Classical School and Whitefield Seminary patiently
endured earlier incarnations of these ideas and helped to shape
them into their present form.

Snippets of this material and earlier versions of these ideas made
their way into innumerable sermons, lectures, and speeches—in
local churches, at Crisis Pregnancy Center banquets, and in
schools, colleges, and universities across the nation. My attentive
audiences helped me reshape the work both through their con-
structive criticism and through their willingness to let me think out
loud. In addition, several of those sermons and speeches eventually made their way into one or another of three anthologies over
the years. I edited two of them myself nearly a decade ago in my
collections, *In the Shadow of Plenty*[3] and *The Changing of the Guard*.[4]
The other one was edited more recently by my friend Howard
Phillips in the collection, *The Next Four Years*.[5] Again, innumerable
correspondents and critics have helped me to dramatically recon-
figure those expositions, illustrations, and applications in both
content and context. Those earlier raw oral transcriptions have
thus been transformed into integral aspects of this, my life's message.

The soundtrack for this project was provided by J. S. Bach,
W. A. Mozart, and Johann Strauss with backup vocals by Steve

Green, Susan Ashton, and Out of the Grey. Meanwhile the midnight musings were provided by Mel Bradford, Andrew Lytle, Colin Thubron, Ellis Peters, Tom Clancy, and P. D. James.

Phil and Sally Bartels gave me the run of their marvelous Victorian "castle" in New Hampshire during the final few days of intensive writing on the first draft. In addition, the good people of Tri-City Covenant Church and Auburn Avenue Presbyterian Church offered me every benefit of their gracious hospitality— among them I have found homes away from home. Meanwhile back at the ranch, David Clary—who has known me longer and better than anyone—crafted me a home right at home.

To all these I offer my deepest and profoundest thanks.

As always, though, it was my family—my wife, Karen, and our children, Joel, Joanna, and Jesse—that most enabled me to write this very personal exploration of the balanced Christian life. With nary a complaint, they sacrificed many weekends as I struggled to squeeze some writing into an already too hectic schedule:

> I thank my God upon every remembrance of you, always in every prayer of mine for you all making request with joy, for your fellowship in the Gospel from the first day until now; being confident of this very thing, that He which hath begun a good work in you will perform it until the day of Jesus Christ. (Philippians 1:3–6)

In the end, that is perhaps the only justification that matters for any work, on any subject, in any discipline.

Notes

1. G. K. Chesterton, *Orthodoxy* (London: Minerva, 1908), 11.

2. Ibid.

3. George Grant, *In the Shadow of Plenty: Principles of Welfare and Poverty* (Fort Worth: American Bureau of Economic Research, 1986).

4. George Grant, *The Changing of the Guard: Principles of Politics* (Fort Worth: American Bureau of Economic Research, 1987).

5. Howard Phillips, ed., *The Next Four Years: A Vision of Victory* (Franklin, Tenn.: Legacy Communications, 1992).

INTRODUCTION: A FRACTURED WORLD

The sin of egotism always takes the form of withdrawal. When personal advantage becomes paramount, the individual passes out of the community.
Richard Weaver

B y almost any standard, it appears that our culture is now coming apart at the seams. Despite all our prosperity, pomp, and power, the vaunted American experiment in liberty seems to be disintegrating before our very eyes.

According to historian Hilaire Belloc: "It is often so with institutions already undermined: they are at their most splendid external phase when they are ripe for downfall."[1]

According to *The Index of Leading Cultural Indicators*, amidst all our comfort and affluence we have become a nation of mayhem and woe.[2] Crime is up. Educational standards are down. Families are crumbling. Basic virtues are disappearing. Government is less reliable. Scandal is more common. Our communities are sundered by antagonistic interests and competing factions. We are divided racially. We are divided economically. We are divided politically. We are divided culturally.[3]

And things are getting worse with every passing day.

We are witnessing what Arthur Schlesinger calls the "disuniting of America."[4] Or worse, we are in the midst of what Daniel Patrick Moynihan pointedly calls "social and geo-political pandaemonium."[5]

Pundits and prognosticators, critics and commentators, gadflies and curmudgeons, prophets and seers alike agree.

According to George Will, we are suffering from "a kind of slow-motion barbarization."[6] Os Guinness says we have already entered the "time of reckoning."[7] Zbigniew Brzezinski says we are simply "out of control."[8] And Paul Johnson asserts we are ensnared by "a moral and ethical folly" that we appear to be "helpless to correct."[9]

Despite our distress at such notions, the fact that we live in a fractured culture actually comes as no great surprise to most of us. Ours is a fallen world after all.

Instead, what often surprises us—or at least what most often grieves us—is the fact that we live in a fractured church as well. The disuniting of America would not be so frightening if it were not accompanied by a disuniting of the faith.

But it is.

We are more divided today than at any time since the Reformation. We are divided over what is right and what is wrong.[10] We are divided over what is good and what is bad.[11] We are divided over what we should do and what we should not do.[12] And as a result, "absolute confusion" is now our most apt epithet, according to demographer George Barna.[13]

Certainly we have always had our squabbles. Substantial theological differences have "enlivened" relations between Christians since the earliest days. But more often than not, our contemporary divisions have little or nothing to do with dogmatic formulations or creedal disputations—as has always been the case before. The fact is, we hardly know enough doctrine to fight over it—as David Wells has asserted, the modern church has "cheerfully plunged into astounding theological illiteracy."[14]

Instead, our divisions tend to be much less substantial—usually along experiential, methodological, or pragmatic lines.[15] We fight over styles and approaches. We part company over techniques and appearances. We are far less concerned with axiomatic first principles than we are with public poses. We are far less concerned with *what* we say or do than with *how* we say or do it.

Perhaps the most glaring example of this is the stark division between activism and piety in the modern church—the dichotomy between pro-lifers on the one hand and prayer warriors on the other, between those involved in politics and culture and those

involved in church growth and evangelism, between those concerned about the issues of our time and those concerned about the
matters of eternity. Nearly every church in America has felt the
tension of this breach.

The real trouble with the dichotomy, though, is that it is a false
dichotomy.

Activism without deep spiritual resources draws from shallow
wells that soon run dry—it cannot long be sustained. Thus it ceases to be active.

Similarly, piety without forthright cultural action inevitably
capitulates to the prevailing pressures of the world—it cannot exist
in a vacuum. Thus it ceases to be pious.

We cannot be authentically Christian and simultaneously be so
heavenly-minded that we're no earthly good any more than we can
be so earthly-minded that we're no heavenly good. The only possibility for us is to be so heavenly-minded that we do the earth
good. And that demands a substantive lifestyle balance where both
faith and work are operative, where both holiness and service
motivate, where both Word and deed dominate, where the Gospel
is proclaimed in both doctrine and in life.

Nevertheless, in this day of illogical logic and meaningless
rhetoric, false ideologies continue to fracture the faith. Thus the
battle lines in the spiritual and cultural wars of our time remain
unclear and the trumpets sound uncertainly.

In the midst of such circumstances, the incomparable Francis
Schaeffer once asked, "How should we then live?"[16]

This book is an attempt at a partial answer. It is a biblical and
historical reflection on how the supposed tensions between
activism and piety can and should ultimately be resolved in our
lives, in our vocations, and in our callings.

Growing out of an understanding of the covenant lawsuit
sequence in the prophecy of Micah, this book revolves around a
kind of shorthand triad of mandates found there: justice, mercy,
and humility. The first two chapters introduce these mandates,
then the succeeding chapters take each of them up in turn—in two
chapters apiece. Thus, chapter 1 focuses on the Micah Mandate
itself. Chapter 2 deals with the thorny problem of worldliness and
how our faith fits in the context of the earth. Chapter 3 examines
the concept of justice through the twin lenses of law and grace,

while chapter 4 looks at it in light of the inevitable offense of the Gospel. Chapter 5 begins the discussion of mercy with a study of the connection between service and priesthood, and chapter 6 concludes it with an examination of the peculiarity of the Christian calling. The discussion of humility before God begins in chapter 7 with a study of worship and sovereignty, and it concludes in chapter 8 with a profile of the basic devotional disciplines. Chapter 9 returns to the subject of balance via the great Reformation doctrine of the priesthood of believers. Chapter 10 attempts to illustrate how the mandates of justice, mercy, and humility can provoke in us a commitment to genuine obedience. Finally, throughout the text, historical sidebars and application exercises provide practical anchors for any elusively theoretical principles.

Opening each new section are several epigrams from the works of Samuel Johnson and Richard Weaver. Johnson was a brilliant eighteenth-century essayist, lexicographer, and literary critic. Noted for his wit and conservatism, his wisdom is an apt reminder of the philosophical root of Christian balance. Weaver was a renowned twentieth-century philosopher, professor, and best-selling author. Noted for his regionalism and traditionalism, his wisdom is an apt reminder that the philosophy of balance has not yet entirely vanished.

Even a cursory glance at my writing reveals that I am an adherent of a time-honored medieval convention: Throughout this monograph you'll find lists of historical figures, lists of biblical texts, lists of practical applications, lists of authors and their ideas, and lists of movements and trends. Though this is not necessarily a popular form of communication in these abbreviated, get-to-the-point, cut-to-the-chase, modern times, it is nevertheless a critical aspect of my own approach to the question at hand.

Even so, this book was never intended to provide a comprehensive new approach to social theory in the way that the works of Henry Van Til or Phillip Schaff once did. Neither is it intended to point the way to a profound new insight into the devotional disciplines in the way that the works of Charles Hodge or Gardiner Spring once did.[17] Indeed, I have self-consciously drawn from these earlier masterpieces—as I have from the works of Calvin, Knox, Machen, Warfield, Spurgeon, Kuyper, and many others—to restate their conception of the balanced Christian life in the context of our present perilous situation.

I have simply tried to serve as an observer, a reporter. I dared not attempt to offer twelve innovative steps toward cultural recovery or seven new management habits for highly effective churches.

Thus, the best that I can offer you is the tried and true, the old and familiar, the well-trod sod. But then, as J. C. Ryle said long ago: "All heaven and earth resound with that subtle and delicately balanced truth that the old paths are the best paths after all."[18]

Indeed they are.

Notes

1. Hilaire Belloc, *Charles the First* (Philadelphia: Lippincott, 1933), 22.

2. William J. Bennett, *The Index of Leading Cultural Indicators* (New York: Simon and Schuster, 1994), 8.

3. Ibid.

4. Arthur Schlessinger, *The Disuniting of America* (New York: Simon and Schuster, 1993).

5. Daniel Patrick Moynihan, *Pandaemonium* (New York: Oxford, 1993).

6. *Forbes*, 14 September 1992.

7. Os Guinness, *The American Hour* (New York: Free Press, 1992), 4.

8. Zbigniew Brzezinski, *Out of Control* (New York: Scribners, 1993).

9. *Forbes*, September 14, 1992.

10. George Grant, *The Family Under Siege* (Minneapolis: Bethany, 1994).

11. George Grant and Mark Horne, *Legislating Immorality* (Chicago: Moody, 1993).

12. George Grant, *The 57% Solution* (Franklin, Tenn.: Adroit Press, 1993).

13. George Barna, *Absolute Confusion* (Ventura, Calif.: Regal, 1993).

14. David Wells, *No Place for Truth* (Grand Rapids: Eerdmans, 1993), 4.

15. Jerram Barrs, et al. *What in the World Is Real?* (Champaign, Ill.: Communication Institute, 1982).

16. Francis A. Schaeffer, *How Should We Then Live?* (Old Tappan, N.J.: Revell, 1976).

17. Henry Van Til, *The Calvinistic Concept of Culture* (Philadelphia: Presbyterian and Reformed, 1959); Phillip Schaff, *The Principle of Protestantism* (Philadelphia: United Church Press, 1964); Charles Hodge, *Commentary on Romans* (Wheaton, Ill.: Crossway, 1994); Gardiner Spring, *The Obligations of the Bible to the World* (New York: Taylor and Dodd, 1839).

18. J. C. Ryle, *The Old Paths* (London: James Clarke, 1959), vii.

AN IMBALANCING ACT

*Some men please themselves with a constant
regularity of life, and decency of behavior. Some
are punctual in attendance on public worship, and
perhaps in the performance of private devotion. Such
men are not hypocrites; the virtues which they
practice arise from their principles. Their religion
is sincere; what is reprehensible is, that it is partial.*
Samuel Johnson

FROM PILLAR TO POST: BALANCE

Worldview is the most important thing
about a man. . . . The denial of universals
carries with it the denial of everything
transcending experience.
Richard Weaver

I have always been fascinated by high-wire acts. I can still recall vividly the first time I craned my neck up toward the pinnacle of the Big Top to witness a beautiful woman prancing across the wide span of the tent with nothing beneath her but a thin cable. I was transfixed.

I was probably about five years old. My father—finally giving in to my relentless begging—had taken me to the circus to see the "lions and tigers and bears, oh my." The pungent closeness of the sawdust-covered arena floor, the wafting aromas of popcorn and cotton candy, the dazzling sights of clowns on motorcycles, acrobats on horseback, and daredevils in cages with roaring beasts captivated my imagination. I was wide-eyed with wonder. But the moment the high-wire act began, nothing else mattered. Though three rings of furious and fabulous activity played before me, I only had eyes for the daring woman balanced a hundred feet above me.

I was hooked.

For the next several years I learned everything I could about high-wire acts. I followed the amazing careers of the Flying Wallendas—a single family that somehow produced three generations of the greatest performers the circus world has ever known. I collected their stats, figures, and memorabilia as relentlessly as any baseball fan.

Now, I'm not entirely sure what it was that so gripped my imagination. I'd always been just a tad afraid of heights, so it wasn't as if I ever wanted to do what the Wallendas did. Certainly I did not envy the life of a circus performer—even as a youngster I was a committed homebody. Perhaps I simply recognized the phenomenal sense of balance the acts demanded—the ability to avoid the extremes of either left or right, of forward or backward. It seemed as if I was always striving for balance—whether I was learning to ride my bike, or climbing into the highest branches of a tree, or seesawing with friends on the playground. A sense of balance lends grace and agility to almost any activity, and I'd always wanted that. Maybe that is why the Wallendas and their high-wire kith and kin made such an impression on me.

As an adult I have often had to realize how much like a highwire act my daily life tends to be. Again and again I find myself shuffling a hundred urgent tasks, precariously perched high above my circumstances, hanging by what seems to be just a thread— and all without a net.

I feel as if I really ought to have the balance of a Flying Wallenda. And that is no mean feat—especially since this is not a circus act. What I'm trying to balance is my life.

Finding Balance

All of us struggle with the competing concerns of life. How do we juggle our obligations at work with our responsibilities at home? How do we give proportionate weight to the things that we know we *need* to do and the things that we just *want* to do? How do we keep our priorities at the forefront of our daily agenda, even in the face of the tyranny of the urgent? How do we maintain a clearheaded perspective in our fast-paced, willy-nilly, fly-by-the-seat-of-our-pants world?

Like high-wire performers, we need balance. Charles Swindoll has said:

> We need balance between kindness and firmness, between waiting and praying, between working and obeying, between saving and spending, between taking in and giving out, between want-

ing too much and expecting too little, between warm acceptance and keen discernment, between grace and truth. For many folks, the struggle with imbalance is not an annual conflict—it's a daily grind.[1]

Recognized as a cardinal human virtue since the earliest days, balance has been lauded in fable, legend, myth, logic, rhetoric, discourse, and law throughout all of history.[2] Though called by any number of different names—"moderation" by Aristotle, "soberness" by Cicero, "equilibrium" by Seneca, "deliberation" by Plato, "temperance" by Tacitus, "self-control" by Apuleius, and "poise" by Plutarch—balance was universally thought to be an essential character trait of the successful and happy life.[3]

The importance of maintaining a life of balance figures prominently in much of the best literature of the ages as well. From Shakespeare's *Merchant of Venice* to Milton's *Areopagitica*, from Ascham's *Schoolmaster* to Chaucer's *Canterbury Tales*, from Defoe's *Robinson Crusoe* to More's *Utopia*, from Johnson's *Rasselas* to Bacon's *Essays*, balance is portrayed as a kind of saving grace.[4] By it heroes overcame tremendous obstacles, the innocent recompensed the guilty, the weak rose above their oppressors, and the unloved and unlovely found everlasting romance.

> ## Biblical balance is a happy melding of devotion and action, being and doing, patience and passion. It manifests word and deed, faith and works, forgiveness and discipline.

The Bible too commends a life of balance. We are to speak the truth; but we are to speak it in love (Ephesians 4:15). We are to desire neither poverty nor riches; we're to embrace neither fullness nor want (Proverbs 30:7–9). We are to bear one another's burdens; we are to bear our own (Galatians 6:2–5). Salvation is a free gift; good deeds must necessarily accompany it (Ephesians 2:8–10). The eternal Gospel is good news; but it is news of fear and judgment (Revelation 14:6–7). We are to hate the sin; we are to love the sinner (Jude 21–23). We are in the world; we are not of the world (John 17:15–16). Faith is not of works; but without works, faith is dead (James 2:26).

For the Greeks, balance was often little more than a compromised life. For the Romans, it was simply the conservative suppression of wilder urges—a kind of taming of residual barbarian impulses.

But biblical balance is altogether different—not just in degree, but in kind. It entails far more than a happy medium between virtue and vice. It is not just an averaging of two extremes or a New Age *centering* of mind, will, and emotions. It is instead a well-rounded, whole-hearted, fully-integrated life rooted in an unswervingly scriptural worldview.

Unlike the kind of balance lauded in the ancient catalog of common virtues, biblical balance does not depend upon the rigors of self-imposed discipline. Neither is it one-dimensional in its scope. It is an animated lifestyle of symmetry and stability, of equilibrium and equanimity, of imperturbability and unflappability. It is a fruitful harvest of "love, joy, peace, patience, kindness, goodness, faithfulness, gentleness and self-control" (Galatians 5:22–23).

The reason is simple. Biblical balance is a happy melding of devotion and action, being and doing, patience and passion. It manifests word and deed, faith and works, forgiveness and discipline. It carefully integrates the inner life and the outer life. It makes quiet conviction the natural companion of strident confession. It enables the head to coincide with the heart. Without compromising God's grace, it reveres God's decrees. Without suppressing spiritual liberty, it upholds spiritual responsibility.

In other words, it is mature.

And in a day marked by its revolt against maturity, biblical balance is a rare commodity indeed. One-dimensional obsessions control our churches, our discussions, and our lives. A thousand competing programs and projects claim our limited time, attention, and resources.

But it need not be so.

Biblical balance is more practical than pragmatism. It is more thoughtful than rationalism. It is more experienced than existentialism and more romantic than sentimentalism. It is more stable than conservatism and more progressive than liberalism.

A faithful return to that kind of balance could very well be the announcement of hope, the clarion cry for revival, that we so desperately long for today.

A Shorthand Statement

Descriptions of biblical balance take various forms throughout the Scriptures—in terms of duties to God and man, purity and charity, behavior and civility, mission and witness, vocation and discipleship, and fellowship and worship.

Each of these pairs is a shorthand statement—an abbreviated version of a profound truth. None of them was ever intended to be comprehensive. Rather, they capture in plain terms different aspects of the multi-faceted beauty of spiritual maturity. Each has its own emphasis. Each has its own perspective. But each points to the same spiritual fundamental—the very practical, nuts-and-bolts, rubber-meets-the-road conception of biblical balance.

One of the most complete of these partial descriptions is found in the Old Testament prophetic book of Micah:

> He has showed you, O man, what is good. And what does the Lord require of you? To act justly and to love mercy and to walk humbly with your God. (Micah 6:8)

A Call for Balance

In 1917, when American troops were preparing to sail across the seas in order to take to the battlefields of France and Belgium in the First World War, the New York Bible Society asked former president Theodore Roosevelt to inscribe a message in the pocket New Testaments that each of the soldiers would be given. The great man happily complied. And he began by quoting Micah's striking triune call for biblical balance—what he called the "Micah Mandate."[5]

Why this particular passage? Because, he said, "The whole teaching of the New Testament" is actually "foreshadowed in Micah's verse."[6]

In his brief message to the soldiers, he explained:

> Do justice; and therefore fight valiantly against those that stand for the reign of Moloch and Beelzebub on this earth. Love mercy;

treat your enemies well; succor the afflicted; treat every woman as if she were your sister; care for the little children; and be tender with the old and helpless. Walk humbly; you will do so if you study the life and teachings of the Savior, walking in His steps.[7]

Roosevelt believed that the ultimate security of men and nations depended on a faithful adherence to Micah's threefold demonstration of biblical balance: a commitment to justice, a concern for mercy, and a reverent humility before Almighty God. He was certain that even with the deployment of superior forces in superior numbers with superior armaments, the American armies would ultimately be defeated during the war if they took to the field without this kind of spiritual integrity. And he was convinced that if we as individuals and families take only our limited material resources into our daily warfare, we too will be defeated and destroyed.

Several generations earlier, George Washington had recognized the unique applicability of the Micah Mandate to America's corporate life. In one of his final statements to the young nation that he had taken such a pivotal role in establishing, he said:

> I now make it my earnest prayer, that God would most graciously be pleased to dispose us all, to do justice, to love mercy, and to demean ourselves with that charity, humility, and pacific temper of mind, which were the characteristics of the Divine Author of our blessed religion, for without an humble imitation and example in these things, we can never hope to be a happy nation.[8]

Likewise, a half-dozen other presidents laid their hands upon Bibles open at the Micah Mandate as they were sworn into office.[9] Two more quoted it in their inaugurations.[10] At least three others cited the passage in speeches during their terms of office. It is engraved upon at least three prominent monuments or buildings in the nation's capital. And it has been influential in innumerable public lives—from Patrick Henry and Samuel Adams to Claire Booth Luce and Jacob Riis.[11]

Theologians and preachers through the ages as varied as Ambrose, Chrysostom, Tertullian, Origen, Calvin, Whitefield, and Cranfield emphasized its central importance in comprehending the full dimensions of the balanced Christian life.[12]

Charles Haddon Spurgeon, the great Victorian voice of orthodoxy, asserted that the verse "beautifully expounded" the "lavish excellencies" of spiritual maturity—by "testing the authenticity of salvation," divining the "symptoms of spiritual health," and provoking the "deepest conceivable pleasures" in a Christian's walk.[13]

Pastors, presidents, and patriots alike recognized that within this single verse was a world of wisdom. It was for them a benchmark of balance.

A Covenant Lawsuit

This often-quoted, highly-touted Micah Mandate is actually the conclusion of an emotionally charged narrative near the end of the prophecy.

With all the elements of a dramatic courtroom scene, the prophet here describes a kind of covenant lawsuit brought by the Lord against His chosen people. The case is called from the very throne room of heaven (Micah 6:1): "Listen to what the Lord says: 'Stand up, plead your case before the mountains; let the hills hear what you have to say.'" All of creation—from the mountains and hills to the very foundations of the earth—is summoned to hear the evidence and to bear witness to the proceedings (v. 2): "Hear, O mountains, the Lord's accusation; listen, you everlasting foundations of the earth. For the Lord has a case against his people; he is lodging a charge against Israel."

The prosecutor then presents His evidence (vv. 3–5): "My people, what have I done to you? How have I burdened you? Answer me. I brought you up out of Egypt and redeemed you from the land of slavery. I sent Moses to lead you, also Aaron and Miriam. My people, remember what Balak king of Moab counseled and what Balaam son of Beor answered. Remember your journey from Shittim to Gilgal, that you may know the righteous acts of the Lord."

The defendant explores the possibility of a plea bargain (vv. 6–7): "With what shall I come before the Lord and bow down before the exalted God? Shall I come before him with burnt offerings, with calves a year old? Will the Lord be pleased with thousands of rams, with ten thousand rivers of oil? Shall I offer my firstborn for my transgression, the fruit of my body for the sin of my soul?"

Apparently, Israel had wearied of the Lord (v. 3). The charge against her was a very serious one: infidelity. The indictment rest-

ed on four incidents from the people's redemption-history. The
first was their dramatic rescue from slavery in Egypt (v. 4). The
second was the raising up of godly leadership—Moses, Aaron, and
Miriam—during the wilderness wanderings (v. 4). The third was
the reversal of Balaam's curses just as the Israelites were about to
make their way into the Promised Land flowing with milk and
honey (v. 5). And the fourth was the long-awaited crossing over
the Jordan: Shittim was the last east-bank encampment; Gilgal was
the first west-bank encampment (v. 5). In each case, God had
demonstrated His covenant faithfulness. He had brought the people through every danger and supplied their every need. But Israel
had failed to respond in kind. Her love had grown cold.

The King, Judge, and Lawgiver . . .
does not require a gift.
Instead, He wants the giver.

Notice that the defendant readily accepts her guilt, but then she
wonders how reparations might be made. Perhaps burnt offerings?
Maybe yearling calves? Or thousands of rams? Or ten thousand
rivers of oil? Or even the firstborn among her children (vv. 6–7)?

No, the King, Judge, and Lawgiver answers by saying that He
requires something far greater, far more precious than any of these
things. He does not require a gift. Instead, He wants the giver.

> He has showed you, O man, what is good. And what does the
> Lord require of you? To act justly and to love mercy and to walk
> humbly with your God. (Micah 6:8)

The mandate for Israel was clear.

In addressing His fickle covenant people—as opposed to the
lost nations at large—the Lord outlined a basic standard for discipleship. Though obviously not a requirement for salvation, it
appears that the Micah Mandate was intended to be a hallmark of
fealty in the kingdom.

In other words, the Micah Mandate was a precise shorthand
description of the mature life of faith. It was a snapshot of biblical
balance.

And it still is.

As theologian C. E. B. Cranfield asserted, the Micah Mandate is "one of those great Biblical definitions of true religion" that "utterly transcend dispositions or dispensations."[14] In fact, Jesus summed up "the more important matters of the law" by repeating the prophet's triad of virtues (Matthew 23:23), securing them ever after as central paradigms for the balanced Christian life: "Woe to you, teachers of the law and Pharisees, you hypocrites! You give a tenth of your spices—mint, dill and cummin. But you have neglected the more important matters of the law—justice, mercy and faithfulness. You should have practiced the latter, without neglecting the former."

Thus, the Micah Mandate intrudes as a truth, not a tradition; as a fresh idea amidst the swarm of lies and libels in our time. Composed of the three essential virtues of justice, mercy, and humility, the prophet's mandate sunders the topsy-turvy tests that pass for facts in our day.

Justice

The word Micah uses for "justice" is the Hebrew *mishpat*. It literally means "the way prescribed, the rightful action, or the appropriate mode of life." But the definition of the word only tells half the story.

Throughout the Bible *mishpat* is inextricably linked with the principle of righteousness. In more than sixty passages all across the wide span of the Old and New Testaments, the Scriptures make plain that they hold the only legitimate way to secure life, liberty, and the pursuit of happiness. Whether at home, in the community, or among the nations, any attempt to find fulfillment apart from the clearly revealed ethical parameters of goodness, truth, purity, faithfulness, and holiness is utter folly. On the other hand, any people that diligently seeks to do right—to do righteousness—will invariably pursue justice as well. The two simply go together. One cannot be had without the other.

Again and again the refrain sounds:

- This is what the Lord says: "Maintain justice and do what is right, for my salvation is close at hand and my righteousness will soon be revealed" (Isaiah 56:1).

- Righteousness and justice are the foundation of your throne.

Love and faithfulness go before you (Psalm 89:14).

• But let justice roll on like a river, righteousness like a never-failing stream! (Amos 5:24).

Jesus emphasized this same unity between moral purity and judicial integrity throughout His earthly ministry. He made plain that if we are to be His disciples in spirit and in truth, then we have a God-ordained duty to uphold: to be salt and light in the midst of this poor fallen world. We have a mandate to redeem our culture and a commission to disciple all the nations.

We must not make the mistake of imagining a sharp division between the "spiritual" and the "earthly." The Bible asserts that we are to think hard about the nature of Christian civilization, to try to develop biblical alternatives to the inhuman humanism in our society, and to pursue justice in tandem with righteousness.

There can be no outward life if there is no inward life. But, there can be no inward life if there is no outward one either. Justice and righteousness are inseparable.

Gouverneor Morris, the great merchant, lawyer, and planter from Pennsylvania who actually drafted the final version of the Constitution, believed with Alexander Hamilton, Patrick Henry, George Washington, and many of the other framers that in order for the American experiment in liberty to succeed, justice and righteousness had to be "welded together as one in the hearts and minds of the citizenry." He yearned that America ever be steadfast in what he called its "Christian consensus." He said:

> Liberty and justice simply cannot be had apart from the gracious influences of a righteous people. A righteous people simply cannot exist apart from the aspiration to liberty and justice. The Christian religion and its incumbent morality is tied to the cause of freedom with a Gordian knot; loose one from the other and both are sent asunder.[15]

According to the Micah Mandate, true discipleship tolerates no distinction between the inward and outward. It connects the heart and the hand, the soul and the body. That is biblical balance.

> He has showed you, O man, what is good. And what does the Lord require of you? To act justly and to love mercy and to walk humbly with your God. (Micah 6:8)

May we thus ever be able to say with Job, "I put on righteousness as my clothing; justice was my robe and my turban" (Job
29:14).

Mercy

The word Micah used for "mercy" is the Hebrew *chesed*. It literally means "goodness, kindness, loyal deeds, or faithfulness." Once
again, though, there is more here than meets the eye.

In the same way that *mishpat*—or justice—is linked with the
practice of righteousness throughout the Bible, *chesed* is linked with
the exercise of authority. They also are inseparable concepts in the
scriptural scheme of things. Authority cannot be had apart from
mercy.

> The ability to lead a society
> is earned, not inherited. And
> it is earned through faithful,
> compassionate, and merciful service.

The Bible is unflinching in its declaration: If we are ever to
influence our families or our culture to stand for goodness, faithfulness, and kindness, then we must graciously serve the hurts, wants,
and needs all around us. Just as God has shown us mercy, we must
demonstrate mercy to others (2 Corinthians 1:3–7).

In 1929, the Council of Religious Affairs in the Soviet Union
was instructed by Josef Stalin and the Central Committee of the
Communist Party to enforce a comprehensive "ban on charitable
or cultural activities by churches."[16] According to Vladimir
Kharchev, a spokesman for the Kremlin at the time, "The State
cannot tolerate any challenge to its claim on the heartstrings of
the Russian people."[17]

Stalin, Kharchev, and the Soviet leadership apparently understood well the connection between authority and merciful service.
They understood that whoever becomes the benefactor of a people
will ultimately be able to wield all manner of authority with them.

This is one of the most basic principles of the Christian worldview: The ability to lead a society is earned, not inherited. And it

is earned through faithful, compassionate, and merciful service.

Unfortunately, this principle has not been widely understood by the modern church—even by those of us actively involved in the cultural arena.

Servanthood—the ministry of exercising mercy—is a much neglected, largely forgotten Christian vocation today. A coalition of humanists has claimed the moral high ground by championing the causes of the hurting, the poor, and the outcast. A band of bureaucrats, social reactionaries, and judicial activists has won the hearts of the people—despite the impotence and inadequacy of their programs—because they have at least made a *pretense* of mercy.

What a terrible irony. Jesus made it plain that if the Christian community wants to have the authority to speak truth into the lives of the people around us, to give moral vision to our culture, and to ultimately shape civil justice, we must not grasp at the reins of power and prominence. Rather, we must serve. We must live lives marked by mercy.

Money, manpower, and mailing lists—as fine and as important as those things may be—are not the keys to cultural transformation. Expansive user-friendly church facilities and services, high-tech growth management seminars, and demographically-precise niche targeting are not the means to reach this generation. Mercy is.

Jesus was a servant (Luke 22:27). He came to serve, not to be served. He came offering mercy at every turn. Not surprisingly, He called His disciples to a similar life of selfless giving. He called us to be servants. He said, "Whoever wants to become great among you must be your servant" (Matthew 20:27). Another time, He told His disciples, "Be merciful, just as your Father is merciful" (Luke 6:36).

The attitude of all aspiring leaders "should be the same as that of Christ Jesus: who, being in very nature God, did not consider equality with God something to be grasped, but made himself nothing, taking the very nature of a servant" (Philippians 2:5–7).

The fact is, modern men are looking for proof. They want evidence.

Genuine mercy is that evidence. It verifies the remarkable claims of Scripture. It tells men that there is indeed a sovereign and gracious God who raises up a faithful people. It tells men that God then blesses those people and gives them workable solutions to the most difficult dilemmas in life.

Clearly, it is not enough for us to merely believe the Bible. It is not enough to simply assert trust in scriptural problem-solving. It is not enough for us to blithely assert that Jesus is Lord. We must authenticate and validate our claims. In short, we must serve, backing up Word with deed (James 2:14–17).

This is, after all, our Christian legacy. The faithful followers of Christ launched the first hospitals, orphanages, almshouses, soup kitchens, charitable societies, relief agencies, rescue missions, hostels, and shelters. And as a result, it was the faithful followers of Christ who led Western civilization to new heights of freedom and prosperity for nearly two millennia.

Humility

The word Micah uses for "humility" is the Hebrew *tsana*. It literally means "a modest approach, to come appropriate with decorum, or to bring wisely." But like *mishpat* and *chesed* its normal use is perhaps even more telling than its dictionary definition.

Again and again in the Bible, *tsana* is used to describe the proper attitude toward the person of God Himself.

The Christian approach to any issue, or any problem, or any situation, or any circumstance—in fact, the Christian approach to the whole of life—must always be *theocentric*. In other words, it must begin and end with—and ultimately be centered in—the Lord. To attempt any approach to reality without this in view is to invite frustration and failure. God is sovereign. This fundamental truth underlies the Christian worldview. Thus, our lives must be filled with a holy fear and reverence of Him—to the point that everything is thereby affected.

The Bible asserts this truth vehemently:

- The fear of the Lord is the beginning of knowledge, but fools despise wisdom and discipline (Proverbs 1:7).

- Clothe yourselves in humility toward one another, because, "God opposes the proud but gives grace to the humble." Humble yourselves, therefore, under God's mighty hand, that he may lift you up in due time. Cast all your anxiety on him because he cares for you (1 Peter 5:5–7).

Humility is not a popular concept these days. Fernanda Eberstadt, in her brilliant coming-of-age novel *Isaac and His Devils*, captured this sentiment: "Humility has a dank and shameful smell to the worldly, the scent of failure, lowliness, and obscurity."[18]

Worship of Him, fellowship with Him, service to Him, and communion in Him must be the center of any and all other activities.

How different is the biblical perspective. A nation whose leaders are humbled in fear before God will ever be blest (Psalm 115:13). Similarly, families—and even individuals—that walk in humility will be exalted and lifted up in due time (James 4:6).

Thomas Jefferson once asked: "Can the liberties of anyone or any people or any nation be secure, when we have removed the conviction that those liberties are the gift of God?"[19]

The answer from Holy Writ is clearly no. Thus, the *Shorter Catechism of the Westminster Confession* properly begins by asserting that, "The chief end of man is to glorify God and to enjoy Him forever."[20] The English reformers who composed it recognized that the beginning of any serious endeavor must necessarily be rooted in a humble and holy fear of our Gracious and Almighty God. Worship of Him, fellowship with Him, service to Him, and communion in Him must be the center of any and all other activities. Biblical faith is a fear of the Living God. That is its essence.

Rebalancing

In our individual lives and in our culture at large, the profound necessity for justice, mercy, and humility before God—not just one or two of those virtues, but all three—is everywhere apparent. You don't have to look far to see how desperately the world needs the kind of balance the Micah Mandate portrays. Even the greatest gifts, the best advantages, and the finest opportunities are quickly squandered without it.

Thomas Chatterton, for example, was among the brightest orbs in the starry English literary constellation. Byron praised him as "a master of the poetic craft." Coleridge, Shelley, and Keats each acknowledged his "stunning evocative abilities." Walpole ranked him "above Dryden" and perhaps "only second to Shakespeare." Wordsworth dubbed him "the marvelous boy."[21]

Nevertheless, unable to maintain even a minimum of balance in his life, his great promise was squandered.

Early on, Chatterton showed extraordinary gifts. He began to compose songs, ballads, satires, and verses at twelve. When his mother, an impoverished widow, secured his apprenticeship with a Bristol scrivener three years later, he turned his hand to political essays, elegies, criticism, and social commentary.

In 1768, when he was just sixteen, he startled editors, historians, and critics by publishing a brilliant eyewitness memoir of the dedication of an old bridge by ancient Benedictine friars— vividly detailing the pomp and ceremonies of the long-forgotten event. The beautiful account—he told the public—was merely translated from a brittle old manuscript found, with others of like character, in a muniment room over the chapel of a local rural parish house.

In short succession he published a whole series of the papers— historical, theological, and poetical—each exciting the interest of experts and common readers alike. Chatterton said they were written by a fifteenth-century monk, Thomas Rowley. Though most of the medieval academics of the day questioned the authenticity of the manuscripts, their undeniable beauty and stunning maturity made them doubt that a youngster like Chatterton could have manufactured such an elaborate ruse, much less have written such magnificent literature.

So despite their misgivings, several publishers began accepting the precocious young writer's purported translations for their journals and magazines—paying him liberal fees. In colonial America, where attachments to tradition were often even more profound than in Europe, he created a sensation and became quite the celebrity. It soon appeared that he had made both his fame and his fortune.

Chatterton quickly plunged into the rough-and-tumble literary world of the eighteenth century. He frequented the theaters, dressed fashionably, and drank heavily. He boldly rejected the faith of his childhood and embraced a life of defiant worldliness.

He continued to write prodigiously as well—often in dissipated all-night binges. And, though he managed to create an authentic medieval style from a unique combination of his reading and his own invention, his now obviously false insistence that his texts were ancient began to cast a shadow over his character. Eventually he carried his ruse a bit too far. Scholars began to attack Chatterton as a fraud, perhaps even a plagiarist. Reluctantly, publishers began to reject his submissions. Commissions disappeared. And the fickle public rushed on to other, newer fascinations.

As quickly as his star had risen, it fell.

In those days the city of London was anything but hospitable to the virtues of justice, mercy, and humility before God. Though it had been almost entirely rebuilt a century earlier—following the Great Fire of 1660—and had not yet suffered the Dickensian horrors of the Industrial Revolution, the city was dingy, dirty, and crowded. Though the skyline was dominated by the majestic spires of Christopher Wren and the royal residences at St. James, Westminster, and Buckingham, the city of narrow streets, alleyways, and tenement lanes was grim, dismal, and claustrophobic. Many of the historic buildings were in shameful disrepair. The Thames was an open sewer. And the impoverished and dispossessed seemed to haunt every corner. Combined with the perpetually damp and foggy climate, the city was a distressing sight—as many visitors attested at the time.

Worst of all, though, London was gripped by a moral crisis. J. C. Ryle said of the city:

> Dueling, adultery, fornication, gambling, swearing, Sabbath-breaking, and drunkenness were hardly regarded as vices at all. They were the fashionable practices of people in the highest ranks of society, and no one was thought the worse of for indulging in them.[22]

Wilberforce had not yet undertaken the abolition of slavery. Howard had not yet begun to reform the prisons. Raikes had not yet established Sunday schools. And the great eighteenth-century revivalists had not yet had their full effect.

Meanwhile, the churches were awash with modern new philosophies and methodologies that seemed to have little correlation with the Gospel. William Blackstone undertook "to go from

church to church and hear every clergyman of note" in the city.
He reported that he "did not hear a single discourse which had
more Christianity in it than the writings of Cicero."[23] In fact, he
said that it would have been impossible for him to discover, from
what he heard, "whether the preacher was a follower of Confucius,
of Mahomet, or of Christ."[24] It was hardly an environment con-
ducive to biblical balance.

As Chatterton accommodated himself to the intemperance of
the city, his excesses became even more pronounced. Though his
advances and royalties were quickly squandered, he intensified his
dissolute lifestyle. Going without food or sleep for days on end, he
wrote with a tortured passion unequaled in English letters. Then
he would indulge in drinking sprees, carousings, and fierce street
brawls.

Such a sad public spectacle made editors even more reluctant to
publish his work—though it continued to be unimpeachably brilliant. Chatterton simply had exhausted his welcome. Tragically he
had exhausted his body as well. His prolific energy could only last
so long. He never seemed to do anything half-heartedly—whether
in work or in play. His brilliant imbalance drove him from one
extreme to another.

Early one summer morning in 1770, finally weighed down and
worn out by circumstances of his own making, the poetic genius
took his own life.

When the door of his small attic room was broken open the
next day, hundreds of small sheaves of paper—covered with his
florid handwriting—were scattered across the floor. At his small
writing desk was an unfinished lament entitled Balance:

> Stepe by stepe, through lyturgy of deathe in life
> He hast besought sweete release somme-where;
> Tottering ere the brynk of devastation and fyre:
> O, to attayne to such an balance: as to but stande.[25]

It was obvious to all who witnessed the tragic scene that
Chatterton had been desperately searching for balance. He
yearned for the ability to find a place of stability, security, and
stillness where he could stand and not be shaken by his own rag-
ing passions. Sadly, he never found that elusive balance—the balance to merely stand—that he craved. He was just eighteen when

the parish sextons buried him in an unmarked pauper's grave.

The Search Continues

The more things change, the more they stay the same.

At first glance, Chatterton's desperate experience may seem more than a little remote from our own—rather like the sad sagas of rock musicians or Hollywood starlets. In his search for balance he was driven to extremes.

In fact, though, balance seems as out of reach for many of us more sober and conservative moderns as it was to young, impulsive Chatterton. And we, like he, are all too often driven to extremes, even if our extremes are extremely conventional.

Actually, we face many of the same obstacles that Chatterton did. All about us stands the clear testimony of an entire culture fascinated by the bizarre spectacle of an imbalancing act. When we try to make it on our gifts and abilities alone, we are destined to stumble and fall. Like Chatterton, we discover that in this poor fallen world an over-reliance on our most obvious strengths often leaves us vulnerable to our most profound weaknesses. The tragic result, now as then, is the destruction of life and hope.

All the more reason to take up the challenge of the Micah Mandate. All the more reason to visibly authenticate the work of grace within us by a faithful witness without us—demonstrating to all the world the possibility of living well-rounded lives of integrity and balance.

In writing to the young Ephesian church, the apostle Paul underscored the importance of that kind of resolve:

> For it is by grace you have been saved, through faith—and this not from yourselves, it is the gift of God—not by works, so that no one can boast. For we are God's workmanship, created in Christ Jesus to do good works, which God prepared in advance for us to do. (Ephesians 2:8–10)

Paul's message comes through loud and clear: God saves us by grace. There is nothing we can do to merit His favor. We stand condemned under His judgment. His bequest of salvation is completely unearned and undeserved.

But we are not saved capriciously, for no reason and no purpose. On the contrary, "we are God's workmanship, created in Christ

Jesus for good works." We are His own possession, set apart and purified to be "zealous for good deeds." We are to demonstrate the reality of God's grace before a watching world. We are to authenticate God's good providence in our lives.

And that is precisely what the balance of the Micah Mandate enables us to do.

TIPPING THE BALANCE

"He has showed you, O man, what is good. And what does the Lord require of you? To act justly and to love mercy and to walk humbly with your God"
(Micah 6:8).

Since the earliest days of the church, the kind of balance between justice, mercy, and spiritual humility highlighted in the Micah Mandate has been a distinguishing characteristic of the lives of virtually all the heroes of the church. Examples abound:

Basil of Caesarea (330–79) was renowned in his day as a man of encyclopedic learning. He left a promising legal practice at the imperial court to establish a Christian community in Annesi committed to the care of the sick and needy. It was not long before his reputation for justice, mercy, and humility before God reached the farthest edges of the Roman Empire. He was a quick-witted adversary to the heretical Arians, he was a valiant defender of biblical orthodoxy, he had a productive theological pen, and he combined a deep and sincere piety with a tough and realistic practicality. He was responsible for the establishment of the world's first non-ambulatory care hospitals, the criminalization of abortion and infanticide throughout the realm, and liturgical reforms that revitalized the worship of the church for generations. When he died at the age of fifty, he was mourned by believers and unbelievers alike.

As a young woman, *Bathild of Chelles* (631–80) was carried away from her English home by pirates and indentured to the court of Clovis II, ruler of the Frankish kingdom. Her great beauty and piety attracted the attentions of the king, and he made her his wife in 649. Some years later, upon the king's death, Bathild became regent for their eldest son, Chlotar III. Using the powers of her position, she stridently opposed the profligate slave trade and the practices of infanticide, exposure, abandonment, and abortion. She encouraged evangelism among the barbaric Celts, she supported local ministries to the needy, and she helped to bring reform to the old Roman legal code. Her patronage of the arts and commitment to the sciences was notable as was her devotion to the disciplines of the Christian life. Her life of balance served as an inspiration to the emerging French nation—who emphasized justice, mercy, and humility before God long before they embraced liberty, equality, fraternity.

A devoted son of the Scottish Reformation, *Andrew Geddes* (1518–86) was a sterling example of compassion, integrity, and truth during the fierce religious conflicts that wracked his tiny nation throughout the sixteenth century. Converted under the preaching of John Knox, he served as a deacon in that great reformer's church. Taking his cue from the biblical injunction to faithfully demonstrate justice, mercy, and humility before God, he used his office as a force for righteous change: He helped to organize the famed "seasons of prayer" in cottages all across Scotland that so profoundly shaped the character of the times, he pioneered a ministry to abandoned and orphaned children, and he consulted with local magistrates in an effort to bring the standards of jurisprudence in line with scriptural principles of justice. A Latin translation of the widely read book *On the Help of the Poor*, by Jean Louis Vives, left a deep impression on Geddes—so much so that he used the book as a model for his various pro-life and charitable activities. Emphasizing Micah's triad of virtues, Geddes left a mark on his land that is felt to this day.

Dozens of others could be cited throughout the wide span of history: George of Diospolis (d. 304), Cuthbert of Lindisfarne (d. 687), Giles Aegidius (d. 796), Edward the Confessor (d. 1066), Otto Blumhardt (d. 1632), James Ramsay (d. 1789), and J. Hudson Taylor (d.

1905). All portrayed the comprehensive claim of Christ on the totality of their lives by daily seeking to illumine the Gospel with justice, mercy, and humility before God. And each played a significant role in laying the foundations for the most glorious flowering of civilization that the world has ever known.

DEVELOPING A SENSE OF BALANCE

"He has showed you, O man, what is good.
And what does the Lord require of you? To act
justly and to love mercy and to walk humbly
with your God" (Micah 6:8).

Compare the lists of character traits in Galatians 5—the fruit of the Spirit and the work of the flesh. Notice how, in each case, the virtues and vices cross the boundaries of the internal and the external life. How do these apply to Micah's triad of virtues?

Study Christ's allusion to the Micah Mandate in Matthew 23:23. In what ways do justice, mercy, and humble faith portray the "weightier matters" of the law?

Read through the biographies of several of the great heroes of the faith throughout the ages, noting how thoroughly they integrated the virtues of justice, mercy, and spiritual humility into their daily lives. You might even want to keep a small journal record of stories that illustrate each virtue or of quotations that highlight their importance. Discipleship is in many ways an art of imitation, so this kind of exercise is more than just an academic accumulation of historical vignettes; it is part and parcel of our maturation in Christ.

Next, do a serious spiritual inventory of your own life. Make a chart: pro and con. But don't simply compare and contrast yourself with the saints of yore—none of us stacks up very well in that light. Instead, note the ways that you've successfully implemented certain virtues in your Christian walk. Then look for a couple of specific areas where the balanced life still seems to elude you. Seek to apply the lessons you've learned from your victories to your defeats.

Finally, seek out some practical opportunities to bring more wholesome balance to your walk and witness. If you're involved in all kinds of activism, you might want to look for some new ways to strengthen your inner life: a prayer partner, a discipleship group, or a serious Bible study. If you've tipped the scales in the other direction, why not seek to volunteer once a week at the local crisis pregnancy center, serve meals at a homeless shelter, or stuff envelopes and answer phones for a ministry aimed at stemming the tide of pornography in your town? Round out the expression of your faith and exercise your calling beyond the narrow confines of your comfort zone.

Notes

1. Charles Swindoll, *Living Beyond the Daily Grind* (New York: Inspiration Press, 1994), 408.

2. James L. Brewster, *Philosophical Themes in Everyday Life* (New York: Scribner, Welford, and Co., 1870), 43–58.

3. Ibid., 44.

4. Ibid., 56–58.

5. Theodore Roosevelt, *Foes of Our Own Household* (New York: Scribners, 1926), 132.

6. Ibid.

7. Ibid.

8. Evan Davis, *Our Greatest President: The Life and Letters of George Washington* (New York: Bedford, 1891), 366.

9. John Gilliam, *I Do Solemnly Swear: The Place of Public Oaths in American Life and Culture* (Cleveland: Carter-Hone Theological Institute, 1951), 67.

10. Jimmy Carter, *Keeping Faith* (New York: Bantam, 1982), 20.

11. Gilliam, 114–21.

12. Litteratae, XLI:449; Homilies, XI:420; Marcion Agnostes, IV:410; De Principis, III:305; Commentaries, XIV:343; Letters, IV:48; Communio Viatorum, 12:4.

13. *Metropolitan Tabernacle Pulpit*, 1557:505–16.

14. Cranfield, 191.

15. James Carter Braxton, *Gouvernor Morris* (Charleston, S.C.: Braden-Lowell Press, 1911), 101.

16. Hans Bruchner, *The Dawning of Darkness: An Eyewitness Account of the Soviet Debacle* (Los Angeles: Freedom's Light, 1959), 97.

17. Ibid., 99.

18. Fernanda Eberstadt, *Isaac and His Devils* (New York: Viking, 1990), 89.

19. John W. Whitehead, *The Separation Illusion* (Milford, Mich.: Mott Media, 1977), 21.

20. *Shorter Catechism of the Westminster Confession*, 1:1.

21. Daniel Wise, *Vanquished Victors* (New York: Nelson and Phillips, 1876), 78.

22. J. C. Ryle, *Christian Leaders of the Eighteenth Century* (Edinburgh, UK: Banner of Truth Trust, 1978), 18.

23. Ibid., 15.

24. Ibid.

25. Albert Collins, *The Foundations of Romanticism in English Letters* (London: Green and Tottenham, 1926), 77.

IN, OUT, OR OF: WORLDVIEW

All the evils in our now extensive catalogue flow from
a falsified picture of the world which . . . results in an
inability to interpret current happenings.
Richard Weaver

A djacent to Lambeth Palace, just across the Thames from
Westminster, is one of London's most delightful gardens.
Within the tiny churchyard of the St. Mary Parish sits a carefully tended walled plot bursting with color and fragrance. A narrow brick-lined pathway winds through lush beds of forget-me-
nots, polyanthus, and crown imperial fritillaries. What appear to
be haphazard clumps of lilac, viburnum, and philadelphus are
linked to one another by a wide wavy border planted with
alchemilla, nepeta, and several other sturdy plants that I've never
been able to identify. Assorted primroses, lilies, and canterbury
bells bloom in spring, and snapdragons, geraniums, and lavender
show their colors in summer. Along one wall, in front of a magnificent wisteria, is a bed aromatic with herbs—basil, thyme, oregano,
and cilantro. Parsley grows among the hollyhocks, honeysuckle
twists around the roses, and tiger lilies peek through the euphor-
bias. It is a hard-won taste of paradise planted in the midst of a
hustle-bustle urban sprawl.

Though the celebrated English gardens of Hever Castle,
Sissinghurst, or Glyndebourne are certainly more spectacular, this
little parish vicar's garden epitomizes for me all that a garden
ought to be. Its personal scale, its wide-ranging palette, and its

orderly conception portray a distinctly practical vision of both the possibilities and the limitations of our fallen world.

As if to underscore this truth, a little bronze plaque adorning one corner of the garden declares: "A good theology will invariably produce a good garden." The first time I read that I chuckled and quickly dismissed it as just another bit of gardener's hyperbole. But the more I thought about it the more I realized that the plaque's epigram actually conveys a uniquely scriptural worldview.

A good theology is more than the sum of its parts. Although it is composed of certain essential dogmas and doctrines, each of those essentials must also be carefully related to all the others. It sees the crucial connection between the profound and the mundane. Although it wisely attends to the minutest of details, it also remains fully aware of how those details affect the bigger picture. It places as much significance on the bits and pieces as it does on the totals.

A good theology is good for the soul. But it is also good for the world. Its spiritual vision gives vitality to all that it touches—from flower gardens to nation states and cultures—simply because the integrity of that vision depends as much on a balanced biblical worldview as on a solid scriptural understanding. Its attention to heavenly concerns is integrally bound to its fulfillment of earthly responsibilities.

Of course, making that connection between heavenly concerns and earthly responsibilities is never easy. We are all constantly tugged between piety and practicality, between devotion and duty, between communion with God and calling in the world. Like tending a well-groomed garden, honing a balanced biblical worldview involves both the drudgery of daily labor and the high ideals of faith, hope, and love. But the results are always worth the extra effort. A good theology—with its comprehensive worldview— inevitably affects the world for good. A bad theology—with its fragmented worldview—sows only tares. In our day, that fact has been proven again and again.

Worldliness

In his landmark book *A Christian Manifesto*, Francis Schaeffer asserted that "the basic problem with Christians in this country" over the last two generations or more has been that "they have

seen things in bits and pieces instead of totals."[1] The result has
been a kind of hesitant hit-or-miss approach to the dilemmas of
our day:

> They have very gradually become disturbed over permissiveness,
> pornography, the public schools, the breakdown of the family, and
> finally abortion. But they have not seen this as a totality—each
> thing being a part, a symptom, of a much larger problem.[2]

He said that part of the reason for this was:

> They failed to see that all of this has come about due to a shift in
> worldview—that is, through a fundamental change in the overall
> way people think and view the world and life as a whole.[3]

When the subject of worldview comes up, we generally think of
philosophy. We think of intellectual pettiness. We think of ivory-
tower speculation, of thick obscure books, and of logical complex-
ities.

In fact, a worldview is as practical as potatoes. It is less meta-
physical than understanding marginal market buying at the stock
exchange or legislative initiatives in Congress. It is less specialized
than typing a book into a laptop computer or sending a fax across
the continent. It is instead as down to earth as tilling the soil for a
bed of petunias.

The word itself is a poor English attempt at translating the
German *weltanshauung*. It literally means a "life perspective" or "a
way of seeing."[4] It is simply the way we look at the world.

You have a worldview. I have a worldview. Everyone does. It is
our perspective. It is our frame of reference. It is the means by
which we interpret the situations and circumstances around us. It
enables us to integrate all the different aspects of our faith, and
life, and experience.

Alvin Toffler, in his book *Future Shock*, said, "Every person carries
in his head a mental model of the world."[5] This mental model is,
he says, like a giant filing cabinet. It contains a slot for every item
of information coming to us. It organizes our knowledge and gives
us a grid from which to think. None of us is completely open-
minded or genuinely objective. "When we think," said economic
philosopher E. F. Schumacher, "we can only do so because our
mind is already filled with all sorts of ideas with which to think."[6]

These more or less fixed notions make up our mental model of the world, our frame of reference, our presuppositions—in other words, our worldview.

James Sire writes:

> A worldview is a map of reality; and like any map, it may fit what is actually there, or it may be grossly misleading. The map is not the world itself of course, only an image of it, more or less accurate in some places, distorted in others. Still, all of us carry around such a map in our mental makeup and we act upon it. All our thinking presupposes it. Most of our experience fits into it.[7]

A worldview is simply a way of viewing the world.

And the Christian view of the world and all the things of the world is fraught with a sort of gardener's paradox—an appreciation for both the potentials and the liabilities of fallen creation. Of course, it is possible to be a Christian and yet hold a worldview more informed by one's culture than by Scripture. But Scripture does tell us how to think about the world, and it tells us that how a person thinks will influence who he is and how he responds.

We know, for instance, that the world is only a temporary dwelling place. It is passing away, and we live here but for a little while as "foreigners and aliens" (Ephesians 2:19). Our true citizenship is in heaven (Philippians 3:20), and our affections are naturally to be set on heavenly things.

In addition, the world is filled with "hidden snares" (Jeremiah 18:22). In tandem with the flesh and the devil, it makes war on the saints. "The deceitfulness of wealth and the desires for other things come in and choke the word, making it unfruitful" (Mark 4:19).

But Christ overcame the world and then chose us out of the world. Thus, we are not to be conformed to the world, neither should we love the world. Though we once "walked according to the course of the world" (Ephesians 2:2) now we are to keep ourselves "from being polluted by the world" (James 1:27). Indeed, "friendship with the world is hatred toward God" (James 4:4).

Thus, warnings against worldliness, carnal mindedness, and earthly attachments dominate biblical ethics. As Oswald Chambers has said, "The counsel of the Spirit of God to the Saints is that they must allow nothing worldly in themselves while living among the worldly in the world."[8]

But then, that is the problem, isn't it? We must continue to live in the world. We must be "in" it but not be "of" it. And that is no easy feat.

> ## [A Christian worldview] must be engaged in the world. It must be unengaged in worldliness.

And to make matters even more complex, we not only have to live in this dangerous fallen world, but we have to work in it, serve in it, and minister in it. We have been appointed ambassadors to it, priests for it, and witnesses in it.[9] We even have to go to the uttermost parts of it.

The reason for this seemingly contradictory state of affairs—enmity with the world on the one hand, responsibility to it on the other—is simply that "God so loved the world that he gave his one and only Son" (John 3:16). Though the world is "under the control of the evil one" (1 John 5:19), God is "reconciling the world to himself in Christ" (2 Corinthians 5:19). Jesus is the light of the world. He is the Savior of the world. He is the "Lamb of God, who takes away the sin of the world" (John 1:29).

A genuinely integrated Christian worldview must be cognizant of both perspectives of the world—and treat them with equal weight. It must be engaged in the world. It must be unengaged in worldliness. It must somehow unite spiritual concerns with temporal concerns. It must combine heavenly hope and landed life. It must coordinate heartfelt faith and down-to-earth practice.

The Micah Mandate does just that. A vision of life and faith that integrates justice, mercy, and humility before God will cover the whole spectrum of heaven and earth. The high ideals of a biblical worldview vitally connect the head with the hand with the heart, by emphasizing hard-hitting issues, human compassion, and unflinching holiness. A proper worldview establishes the priorities of cultural, interpersonal, and devotional integrity, which are happily instituted by the grace of God.

Back to the Garden

Throughout the story of redemption, Scripture highlights and reinforces this kind of balanced perspective of the created realm in which we live. Whenever and wherever God reveals His purposes for us, He makes clear the connection between the things of heaven and the things of earth. And He does it by illustrating profound spiritual matters in mundane physical terms.

When Adam and Eve were banished from the paradise of Eden, for example, they were not only cut off from God's presence spiritually, they were physically locked out of their garden home as well (Genesis 3:17–24). Their tilling became toiling. Their sin not only ravaged their hearts and souls, it ravaged their situations and circumstances. The supernatural was revealed in the natural. Apparently obscure spiritual realities were expressed in painfully obvious practical experiences.

And the story of Adam and Eve is by no means unique in this regard. Incarnational truth—the spiritual revealed and made manifest in the physical—is the very nature and essence of biblical revelation.

An integral aspect of the covenant God made with Abraham, for instance, was the promise of a garden-like inheritance. Abraham was promised land. Though "he was looking forward to the city with foundations, whose architect and builder is God" (Hebrews 11:10), he was given a glimpse of that heavenly hope in the very earthly realms of the Canaanites, Amorites, and Jebusites (Genesis 15:18–21).

When Moses and the children of Israel came up out of the bondage of Egypt, they too sought "him who is invisible" (Hebrews 11:27). But the invisible rewards of a world yet to come were illustrated for them by the visible blessings of a world already here. Thus, they went forth to claim a promised land—a bounteous garden flowing with milk and honey.

Jeremiah, even when he knew judgment was imminent and his own fate was grim, bought a garden plot as an inheritance for his family (Jeremiah 32:6–15). The hope of divine deliverance in the future was vividly and objectively portrayed in a real estate transaction.

Christ even described the proclamation of the Gospel in very earthly terms: It is seed sown upon the soils, wheat amidst the tares, a tract white unto harvest, a ripened vineyard, and a treasure in a field.

A balanced biblical worldview takes all this into account. It recognizes that though this world is corrupted and defiled, we need to care for it as a garden. Until God takes us out of this world, our lives—physical and spiritual—are inescapably tied to it. Thus, the just society of a righteous people is invariably portrayed in the Bible as a "well-watered garden" (Isaiah 58:11). Though we do not yet live in the "better country" of our eternal hope, we are nevertheless to responsibly tend earth (Hebrews 11:16). Only as we understand this redemptive link between heaven and earth can we ever hope to comprehend the glorious provisions and purposes of grace. Only as we forge a biblical worldview can we fathom the intentions of God's good providence in His creation.

The Great Commission

God has not limited the jurisdiction of His sovereignty to heaven. "The earth is the Lord's" (Psalm 24:1). That is clear enough. At the same time, though, He graciously apportions it out to His people. He commissions us to exercise stewardship over it. We are to be more than just salt: preserving. Our mission includes being light: reclaiming. Justice, mercy, and humility before God need to be balanced virtues in our lives as we reach out to a lost and dying world.

This is the crux of a balanced biblical worldview. And Christ dramatically underscored it in His final instructions to His disciples in the Great Commission. He said:

> All authority in heaven and on earth has been given to me. Therefore go and make disciples of all nations, baptizing them in the name of the Father and of the Son and of the Holy Spirit, and teaching them to obey everything I have commanded you. And surely I will be with you always, to the very end of the age. (Matthew 28:18–20)

All authority in heaven is His, of course. The heights and the depths, the angels and the principalities are all under His sovereign rule. But all authority on earth is His as well. Man and creature, as well as every invention and institution, come under His sovereign rule. There are no neutral areas in all of the cosmos that escape the authority of the Lord Jesus Christ (Colossians 1:17).

Therefore, on this basis, the Great Commission states that

believers are to extend Christ's kingdom, making disciples in all nations by going, baptizing, and teaching. This mandate is the essence of the New Covenant, which is but an extension of the Old Covenant: Go and begin the process of reclaiming everything in heaven and on earth for His name's sake (Genesis 1:28).

> # We need to make disciples who will obey everything that He has commanded, not just in a hazy zone of piety, but in the totality of life.

The emphasis is inescapable: We are not to stop with simply telling the nations that Jesus is Lord; we need to demonstrate His lordship in our families, in our churches, in our work, in our communities, and in our culture. We need to make disciples who will obey everything that He has commanded, not just in a hazy zone of piety, but in the totality of life.

This is the thrust of the Great Commission. We have been given the spiritual, emotional, and cultural mandate to win the world for Jesus. And though we know that only Christ Himself can fulfill that mandate in its entirety at the close of human history, our duty is to trust and obey Him.

The tendency of many modern Christians to sidestep all the implications of the Great Commission except soul-saving has, unfortunately, paved the way for inhuman humanism's program to afflict the helpless, crush our liberties, and despoil our culture. When the Christian's task is limited to snatching brands from the flickering flames of perdition, then virtually all Christian influence is removed from the world. There is little or nothing to restrain the ambitions of evil men and movements. There are no checks, no balances, no standards, and no limitations. God's counsel goes unheard and unheeded.

Commenting on this tragic tendency, Charles Haddon Spurgeon said:

> There are certain pious moderns who will not allow the preacher to
> speak upon anything but those doctrinal statements concerning the

way of salvation which are known as "the Gospel." We do not stand
in awe of such criticism, for we clearly perceive that our Lord Jesus
Christ himself would very frequently have come under it. Read the
Sermon on the Mount and judge whether certain among the pious
would be content to hear the like of it preached to them. Indeed,
they would condemn it as containing very little Gospel and too
much good works. They would condemn it as containing all too
much of the legal. But we must never let be forgotten Christ's
emphasis: the law must be preached, for what the law demands of
us, the Gospel produces in us, else ours is no Gospel at all.[10]

A biblical worldview, as Spurgeon asserts, embraces the comprehensive implications of the Great Commission. It applies
Scripture to every area of life and godliness. The salvation of souls
is the immediate aim of the Great Commission. But the more ultimate aim is the promotion of the glory of the Triune God (Romans
16:25–27). We must have a passion for souls (2 Corinthians 5:11).
We must take every opportunity, expend every energy, and risk
every expense beseeching men to be reconciled to God
(2 Corinthians 5:20). But individualistic redemption is not the do-
all and end-all of the Great Commission.

Thus, our evangelism must include sociology as well as salvation; it must include a new social order as well as a new birth; it
must include reform and redemption, culture and conversion, a
reformation as well as a regeneration. Read the sermons of the
great evangelists through the ages, and you will immediately see
that kind of balance—they invariably begin by addressing the
grave injustices of the day, proceed to examples of human need,
and conclude with a vital appeal to reconcile with Christ.
Regardless of the text, the outline is simple: justice, mercy, and
humility before God.

Any other kind of evangelism is shortsighted and impotent. Any
other kind of evangelism fails to live up to the comprehensive high
call of the Great Commission. Our culture attests all too well that
our niche group, church growth, twelve-step recovery, and least-
common-denominator strategies are simply not sufficient for the
task of satisfying that kind of world vision. It is therefore high time
to release our evangelism from the restraints of a partial and passive
Christianity in order to mount a full-scale assault on the evil and privation of the dominions of darkness. It is high time we set our evan-

gelistic visions by the broad-spectrum scriptural pattern. It is high time evangelism becomes the invasion of heart and soul, of life and liberty, and of land and faith it was intended from the start to be.

The Big Picture

The people of Israel seemed to drift to one of two extremes. Either they were terribly spiritual to the neglect of their earthly responsibilities, or they were terribly worldly to the neglect of their faith (Micah 3:8–11). Either way, the people were prone to see things in "bits and pieces" rather than in "totals" (3:12). They decried the prophet's clear message of faithful balance and integration, saying, "Do not speak out" (2:6 NASB).

As a result, their culture was completely awash in disarray, confusion, and debauchery (Micah 2:8–11). They were at risk of losing their covenantal inheritance—and their promised land (1:9).

The whole point of the Micah Mandate was to shatter their imbalance and tendency toward extremes. Honoring it would bring solid biblical balance to their lives. Micah saw their tendency to view earthly and spiritual concerns with an "either/or" mindset, which he wanted to replace with a fully integrated "both/and" worldview.

But then, imbalance is precisely what the Micah Mandate guards against. It affords us balance, not through compromise, but through a righteous commitment to walk in accord with God's providential working in the world. It equips and enables us to be "in" the world but not "of " it.

This principle runs all through the Bible. God's redemptive work involves more than saving souls. It involves more than preserving the status quo. It involves making "all things new" (2 Corinthians 5:17).

A Balanced Worldview

Forging a genuine Christian worldview—one that integrates a proper concern for this fallen world and simultaneously maintains true spirituality—is no easy bill to fill. But then, neither is it impossible. In fact, history books are filled with the inspiring stories of men and women who faithfully and diligently hammered out that kind of balance in the context of their lives and work.

Patrick Henry, for instance, was not only a great American patriot, he was a man of profound faith who took seriously the call to view all things through the lens of Scripture. There can be little doubt that he strove to maintain the balance that only a biblical worldview can afford. He lived out the Micah Mandate.

On the fourth day of the Second Virginia Convention, Henry kindled the fires of the American Revolution with blazing words that would forever alter the course of this continent:

> Is life so dear, or peace so sweet, as to be purchased at the price of chains and slavery? Forbid it, Almighty God. I know not what course others may take, but as for me, give me liberty or give me death.[11]

As he spoke, all the greatest luminaries of the day were present—Washington, Jefferson, Randolph, Harrison, Wythe, Braxton, and Lee—but Henry would later say that he was actually only concerned to please one witness to his oratory that day—Almighty God.

That insight helps to explain how and why Henry devoted himself to public affairs throughout his life. He was, after all, a devout Christian—and thus fell under no illusions about the relative significance of temporal affairs in the light of eternity. As a committed family man, he was keenly aware of the intrusion of public concerns into private duties. And as a southern agrarian he was decidedly diffident about the cosmopolitan diversions of civic involvement. Like so many of the other revolutionary leaders of his day, the most notable aspect of Patrick Henry's character was that he was not particularly revolutionary. A profoundly conservative man in both manner and resolve, he was loathe to indulge in any kind of radicalism that had the potential to erupt into violence—rhetorical, political, or martial. He was a faithful son of the colonial gentry devoted to the time-honored conventions of Whig representative covenantalism: the rule of law, unswerving honor, and the maintenance of corporate order. He believed in a tranquil and settled society free of the upsets and tumults of agitation, activism, and unrest.

In short, Patrick Henry was very much a man of his time and place.

He was second of eleven children—descended from solid Scottish Presbyterian stock. He worked hard—as a planter, a shop-

keeper, and a country lawyer. In addition he was the primary edu-
cator of his children—teaching them Greek, Latin, Logic,
Rhetoric, History, and Classical Literature. And as if that weren't
enough, he kept himself busy in his work as a church vestryman, as
the sponsor of several missions to the frontier, as a some-time dele-
gate to the House of Burgesses, and as an informal rotating instruc-
tor at a local Presbyterian meeting house.

He was too busy with the ordinary responsibilities of life to
involve himself in radical politics. His deeply ingrained Christian
faith would not allow him to be distracted from what he called
"those essential permanent things."12

In that regard, he was not alone, of course. The reticence of virtually all the notable colonials to squabble with the crown or to
dally in political petulance was obvious to even the most casual
observer. They exhausted every recourse to law before they even
thought to resort to armed resistance. For more than a decade they
sent innumerable appeals, suits, and petitions to both parliament
and the king. Even after American blood had been spilled, they
refrained from impulsive insurrection.

It took more than the Boston Massacre, more than Lexington
and Concord, more than Bunker Hill, more than Falmouth, and
more than Ticonderoga to provoke the patriots to commit themselves to forceful secession. Even as late as the first week of July
1776, no solid consensus among the members of the Continental
Congress felt that "such an extreme as full-scale revolt," as John
Dickinson dubbed it, was necessary. That week, the delegates vot-
ing on the Declaration of Independence defeated it twice before
they diffidently adopted it—and even then they managed to keep
its pronouncements secret for four more days. And though Patrick
Henry was an early advocate of independence, he did not arrive at
that conviction easily or casually.

Like virtually all his fellow patriots he was, at best, a reluctant
revolutionary.

Why then did he rebel? What could possibly have so overcome
his native conservatism? Why would such a naturally taciturn man
seek to rouse his comrades to insurrection—however valiant the
cause?

His abiding Christian worldview—his commitment to those
lasting things, both in heaven and on earth, that transcend the

ever-shifting tides of situation and circumstance—finally drove him to action. He resolved to challenge king and motherland in order to preserve all that which king and motherland had always represented before: justice, mercy, and humility before God.

Henry actually abhorred worldly affairs, but he was thrust into the affairs of the world. His ultimate concern was the world into which he would someday go, but he devoted much of his career to the world into which he had already come. He forged a practical balance between the temporal and eternal as the best expression of Christian faithfulness.

Our ultimate purpose must never be to "change the culture" but to honor the living God.

Patrick Henry had his priorities straight. His worldview was sound. His passion for justice—which made him an oratorical firebrand—was carefully balanced by an equal passion for mercy and spiritual humility—which made him a statesman rather than just a politician.

All too often we fall into the trap of focusing on one virtue to the exclusion of all the others. The sad result is that our virtues practically become vices. Thus, when we emphasize justice without mercy, we develop hard heads and even harder hearts. When we emphasize mercy without justice, we develop soft heads and even softer hearts. When we emphasize either one without humility, we develop a kind of spiritual megalomania—thinking that our project, or our focus, or our methodology is the best and only way. We're either so heavenly-minded that we're no earthly good, or so earthly-minded that we're no heavenly good.

Patrick Henry avoided those traps. He apparently understood that while he was a citizen of one kingdom, he was an ambassador to another. Each role was important. In fact, the roles were essentially inseparable in his mind—the flip sides of a single coin— though he knew that the former determined the latter. He understood that he was to be "in the world" but not "of it." Thus his allegiance to Christ was made manifest just as much in his earthly responsibilities as in his heavenly ones. The integration of justice, mercy, and humility before God was woven into the very fabric of his life and faith. It was the warp and woof of his worldview.

Micah's Worldview

The modern church is sundered by activists who want to save the world on the one hand and by pietists who want to ignore it on the other. Both perspectives are tragically out of sync with the kind of balanced biblical worldview Patrick Henry and a myriad of other faithful Christians in the past attempted to live by.

Our protests, letter-writing campaigns, legal initiatives, and moral crusades will never save the world. Our struggle for political legitimacy, our attempts at media savvy, and our cultural trench warfare will never "take America back." As Michael Scott Horton has aptly asserted: "We are going to have to realize that America is a mission field, not a battlefield."[13] The church is not just another interest group or political action committee. Our goals must never be set by the standards of this poor fallen world—either positively or negatively. Our ultimate purpose must never be to "change the culture" but to honor the living God. That we all too often lose sight of that fact is shameful.

But neither detachment nor irrelevance honors God. An ethereal and pious disassociation from the great questions of our day is not Christian single-mindedness; it is gnostic absent-mindedness. To be so heavenly-minded that we are no earthly good does not only present a poor witness to the transforming power of the Gospel before a watching world, it neglects the pattern of discipleship before the hosts of heaven. The abhorrence of the Gospel by those who control the cultural apparatus in our day is not nearly so frightening as the abhorrence of responsibility by those who inhabit the vast evangelical ghetto. The former is simply evidence of the fallen estate, while the latter bespeaks indifference in the face of grace. That too is shameful.

We are not to be of the world. But neither are we to be out of it. Both extremes malign God's intentions for us and those whom God has placed around us. Both obscure the divine imperative to live justly, love mercy, and walk humbly with our God. Both obliterate a biblical worldview. Both impede us from tending the garden of this world and yield it up to the ravages of a howling wilderness.

Our present challenge is therefore as clear as the challenge that faced Patrick Henry so very long ago—and indeed that has faced every generation of believers since the day of Pentecost: "How long therefore will you waver between two opinions? If the Lord is God, follow him" (1 Kings 18:21).

FROM WASTELAND TO GARDEN

*"He has showed you, O man, what is good. And
what does the Lord require of you? To act justly and
to love mercy and to walk humbly with your God"*
(Micah 6:8).

Through the ages, Christian heroes were invariably able to recognize that though they were not to be of the world, neither were they to be out of it. Time after time, they portrayed a distinctively balanced biblical world-view. They approached the wasteland of this world with all the intensity of determined gardeners. Examples abound:

Boniface of Crediton (675–754) spent the first forty years of his life in quiet service to the church near his home in Exeter. He discipled young converts, cared for the sick, and administered relief for the poor. He was a competent scholar as well, expounding Bible doctrine in a small theological center and compiling the first Latin grammar in England. But in 718, Boniface left the comfort and security of this life to become a missionary to the savage Teutonic tribes along the Germanic frontier. When he was well over seventy, he and his companions were set upon by heathen Frieslanders and put to the sword. But while the attackers were able to snuff out his life, they could do nothing to stifle his influence. He affected virtually every aspect of life in medieval Germany—from educational institutions and political structures to worship services and evangelistic outreaches. His worldview was all-encompassing, and as a result his influence was all-embracing.

The beautiful and beguiling *Elizabeth of Bratislava* (1207–31) was the daughter of the Hungarian king,

Andrew II. Her marriage at the age of fourteen to
Ludwig of Thuringia, though arranged for political reasons, was a happy one, and the couple had three children. In 1227, Ludwig died suddenly after joining a
band of crusaders bound for the Holy Land. Grief-
stricken for some months, the young Elizabeth finally
vowed to give the rest of her life in service to the needy.
She helped establish one of the first foundling hospitals
in Europe, as well as several orphanages and almshouses.
Justice and mercy were the hallmarks of her worldview,
but they were defined by the parameters of humility and
faith. Though her life was short, her legacy endures
both in heaven and on earth.

Charles Haddon Spurgeon (1834–92) is commonly heralded
as the greatest preacher to grace the Christian pulpit
since the apostle Paul. His Metropolitan Tabernacle was
undoubtedly a dynamic force for righteousness in
Victorian England. But his many years of ministry were
marked not only by his masterful pulpiteering, but by
his many social and cultural labors as well. In 1861, he
erected an almshouse for the elderly. In 1864, he established a school for the needy children of London. In
1866, he founded the Stockwell Orphanages. And in
1866, to these many enterprises he added still another, a
private hospital. In all he was responsible for some sixty
different institutions—schools, seminaries, colportage
societies, missionary agencies, and mercy ministries. His
commitment to fulfilling the Great Commission led him
to a fully integrated and dynamically engaged worldview—and ultimately established him as a paragon of
balanced and effective evangelical leadership.

Dozens of others could be cited throughout the wide
span of history: Giles of Aegidius (d. 796), Clement
Slovensky (d. 916), Edburga of Winchester (d. 960),
Louis of France (d. 1270), Benedict the Black (d. 1657),
Edward Ridley (d. 1699), and Charles Wesley (d. 1788).
Each sought to develop a biblical worldview distinguished by a commitment to justice, mercy, and humility before God. And thus each tended the garden of this
world carefully and with discernment.

LIVING WORLDVIEWISHLY

"He has showed you, O man, what is good.
And what does the Lord require of you? To act
justly and to love mercy and to walk humbly
with your God" (Micah 6:8).

Read the apostle Paul's very practical instructions in Romans 12. Notice the comprehensive nature of these guidelines for a full-orbed Christian lifestyle—covering everything from societal issues and interpersonal relationships to care for the brethren and solace for the soul. How might the Micah Mandate induce this kind of balanced worldview perspective?

Discernment is one of the weakest links in the modern church. So, why not hone your discerning powers? Play a little game of "Identify the Worldview" with a friend. Here's how it works: Start naming some of today's hottest trends, or ideas, or books, or movies, or songs, or fashions and then see if you can identify the worldview orientation that each one represents. What about television programs? Or ads and commercials? How do they differ from a Christian worldview? Why?

Now read a couple of the classics from Christendom's past: Chaucer, Shakespeare, Milton, Johnson, or Scott. How do the worldviews of these works differ from the current crop of cultural expressions? How might these differences affect us all—even in subtle, unconscious ways?

An old computer-programming adage asserts "garbage in, garbage out." If our only cultural input is contrary to the worldview that we wish to inculcate, there is little chance that we will reflect anything other than contrarian views. Thus, we all ought to try to develop a conscious program of alternative cultural stimuli. Read the classics. Listen to fine and uplifting music. Turn off the television—or better yet, put it out in the garage. Rebuild your worldview from the foundations up.

Notes

1. Francis Schaeffer, *A Christian Manifesto* (Wheaton, Ill.: Crossway, 1981), 17.

2. Ibid.

3. Ibid.

4. E. F. Schumacher, *Small Is Beautiful* (New York: Harper & Row, 1975), 52.

5. Alvin Toffler, *Future Shock* (New York: Bantam, 1971), 158.

6. Schumacher, Small, 52.

7. James Sire, *How to Read Slowly* (Wheaton, Ill.: Harold Shaw, 1978), 14–15.

8. Oswald Chambers, *Biblical Ethics* (Ft. Washington, Pa.: Christian Literature Crusade, 1964), 35.

9. 2 Corinthians 5:20; 1 Peter 2:9; Matthew 24:14.

10. Harold Latternic, *Spurgeon and Society* (London: New Baptist Union, 1981), 33.

11. Harold G. Lee, *Henrico Parish* (Richmond, Va.: Landmark, 1978), 11.

12. Ibid., 12.

13. Michael Scott Horton, *Beyond Culture Wars* (Chicago: Moody, 1994), 263.

JUSTICE: TO DO RIGHT

Virtue is the highest proof of understanding,
and the only solid basis of greatness. . . .
Therein lies the hope of justice.
Samuel Johnson

LEGAL ENTANGLEMENTS

*To establish the fact of decadence is
the most pressing duty of our time.*
Richard Weaver

W
e arranged to meet in a bookstore. Naturally. Tom Gilmore and I had been corresponding for more than eighteen months—ever since he saw a book review I had written in a literary magazine. He had read the book—a blatantly liberal and humanistic analysis of the American judicial system under the Bush administration—and was taken aback by my rather positive critique.

"How could you?" he had complained.

I wrote back explaining how I could. And thus began a very unlikely friendship.

I rode one of the famous streetcars down Market Street and then crossed through China Town on foot. The sights and sounds and smells of San Francisco in the spring are nearly indescribable. The rugged hills and glistening bay combine with the sophisticated bustle of street life and the aromas of some of the world's best cuisine to create an incongruously delightful texture to a supremely urban setting.

I was headed toward one of my favorite places in the city, the City Lights Bookstore. Since the fifties it has been a popular literary meeting place for artists, writers, students, radicals, bibliophiles, and tourists. Over the years it has played host successively to the Beatniks, the Peaceniks, the Hippies, the Yippies, and the Yuppies. It is colorful and eccentric.

It is also a great bookstore. Its shelves hold an unparalleled selection of poetry and fiction. Though a little slanted toward leftist revisionism, its history section is quite vast. And its modern philosophy department is as complete as any I have seen. But its section devoted to the subjects of law, justice, and politics amazes me most.

When Tom caught up with me, that is where I was.

The selections before us ran the ideological gamut—from unrepentant communism to wild-eyed anarchism. Books advocated everything from a revived Fascism to a refurbished Stalinism. Even the "mainstream" treatises on American legal theory seemed to cover the whole judicial waterfront: Positivism, Determinism, Rationalism, Reductionism, Strict Constructionism, Loose Constructionism, Progressive Constructionism, and Organic Constructionism were all well represented.

"I don't know how anyone could ever sort all this out," Tom commented, amazed. "I always thought that there were just two varieties of politics: liberal and conservative. But it appears that justice can mean almost anything to anybody."

"In some ways, error is infinite in its variety," I replied. "But truth is always uniquely singular. At the same time, though, all of these ideological formulas seem to gravitate toward either extreme legalism or extreme lawlessness. In the end, all the high-sounding rhetoric and the noble political sloganeering boils down to this: We either tend to believe that a strict adherence to some system of law will save us, or we believe that no system of law really matters or is binding upon us. These polar opposites are nevertheless identical in their ideological rigidity."

For months I had been challenging Tom to rethink his adamant ideological bent. He had gone from one extreme to another since his conversion a couple of years earlier—from hard-core liberalism to reactionary conservatism. I tried to show him that the two positions were just flip sides of the same coin—that both depend upon an inherently imbalanced view of the law.

"Non-Christian systems of law and justice invariably fall into this twin trap of legalism and lawlessness," I said, sweeping my hand across the shelves in front of us. "The only possible alternative to this Babel-like confusion is a return to biblical fidelity."

"And that's neither exclusively conservative or liberal," he surmised.

"That's right," I said. "It's neither. It's entirely non-ideological. The rarest of all notions in these difficult days in which we live."

Faith, Hope, and Politics

And now abide faith, hope, and politics, these three; but the greatest of these is politics. Or so it seems.

In the twentieth century, the smothering influence of partisan ideology is everywhere evident. It has wrested control of every academic discipline, every cultural trend, every intellectual impulse, even every religious revival in our time. From Nazism and Stalinism to Pluralism and Multiculturalism, from Liberalism and Conservatism to Monopolism and Socialism, ours has been an epoch of movements beguiled by the temporal seductions of ideological politics.

In a nutshell, that is what Tom and I witnessed in that bookstore in San Francisco.

Nearly every question, every issue, every social dilemma has been and continues to be translated into legal, juridical, or mechanical terms. They are supplied with bureaucratic, mathematical, or systemic solutions. If something is wrong with the economy, then government must fix it. If family values are absent, then government must supply them. If health-care provision is inefficient, then government must rectify the situation. If education is in disarray, then government must reorder the system. Whatever the problem, it seems that law is the solution.

Virtually all social historians agree that this is the most distinctive aspect of our age: the subsuming of all other concerns to the rise of political mass movements based upon comprehensive, secular, closed-universe intellectual systems. Thus, many modern writers have dubbed this the "Age of Ideology."[1]

The name of the ideological game is power. That power may be obtained by imposing the strict standards of law over the totality of life, or it may be obtained by the obliteration of all legal obligations. But either way, the object is power.

In short, an ideological approach to law and justice is little more than humanism rooted in the politicization of every detail of life.

It is a worldview as thorough and as dominating in our time as was the Faith during the epoch of Christendom. And it plunges us into the maelstrom of the twin perils of legalism and lawlessness with a hearty abandon. As a result, any discussion of justice is apt to become bogged down in the mechanical details of legal management, regulation, and enforcement. Talk about justice and people expect political partisanship, policy pronouncements, administrative agendas, and strategic systems. It has been reduced to one or another of a myriad of laws to pass, cases to try, or sentences to impose.

But this modern notion is a far cry from the biblical vision of justice that the American founders and pioneers maintained. They did not trust legal systems to solve the problems that afflicted individuals, communities, and societies. Certainly they believed in strong and active civil constructions for justice—but only in their proper place. Thus they abhorred every brand of ideology. They worked for justice, but they did not believe law was the ultimate good.

Thomas Jefferson warned against the danger of "reducing the society to the law or the law to society."[2] Patrick Henry argued that the contention that the systemic legal structures should intrude into and exercise control over the family and the household was a "great and pernicious error."[3] Gouvenor Morris insisted that the everyday affairs of society should be designed to avoid what he called the "interference of the law beyond its competence."[4]

The problem is, even Christians are prone to fall into the twin traps of ideology. We either overemphasize the importance of law and justice, or we ignore it altogether. We either become obsessed with systemic legalism, or we flirt with a kind of licentious liberty.

Either way, authentic justice no longer operates in our lives and our world.

Legalism

With an obvious sense of sober grief, the apostle Paul wrote to the small community of believers in Galatia:

> I am astonished that you are so quickly deserting the one who called you by the grace of Christ and are turning to a different

gospel—which is really no gospel at all. Evidently some people are throwing you into confusion and are trying to pervert the gospel of Christ. But even if we or an angel from heaven should preach a gospel other than the one we preached to you, let him be eternally condemned! As we have already said, so now I say again: If anybody is preaching to you a gospel other than what you accepted, let him be eternally condemned! (Galatians 1:6–9)

Somehow the Christians in the Galatian church had been "bewitched" (Galatians 3:1). They had fallen into the grips of the most ancient heresy: salvation by law.

Galatia was a huge Roman province in the central mountainous region of Asia Minor. On his first missionary journey, the apostle Paul had founded a number of churches there: in Antioch, in Iconium, in Lystra, and in Derbe. Later he would make at least two follow-up visits, so that the entire region was evangelized and "the word of the Lord spread widely and grew in power" (Acts 19:20).

Shortly after Paul's departure, however, a number of Jewish teachers arrived in Galatia. Whereas Paul had taught salvation "by grace through faith" and this alone, these men insisted that non-Jewish converts must also be circumcised and observe all the minutia of the law in order to be saved. They contradicted Paul and the message of the Gospel, saying that faith is not enough; we must merit God's grace.

The Galatians believed this twisted doctrine despite the fact that the whole of the Bible—from Genesis to Revelation—is diametrically opposed to it. Legalism is heresy. It is an Old Testament heresy and a New Testament heresy. It was condemned by Isaiah, Amos, and Habakkuk. David exposed the futility of salvation by works no less vehemently than did Paul, John, Jude, or Peter.[5]

Legalism abolishes the significance of the cross. It makes light of Christ's sacrifice. It nullifies the work of the Holy Spirit. It abrogates the necessity of grace.[6] "Faith is made void and the promise is nullified" (Romans 4:14) because it makes man and man's ability the measure of all things rather than the rule of God (Matthew 15:6–9).

Salvation according to the Bible is a work of grace. There is nothing we can do to merit God's favor (Ephesians 2:4–9).

People from all walks of life, in every age, on every continent have always attempted to avoid the implications of salvation by grace alone. None of us can stand the thought of being at the mercy of God. And so we constantly dream up new versions of the same old heresy: salvation by works, salvation by law, salvation by education, salvation by legislation.

The Galatians had fallen under the sway of this heresy and thus were "preaching another Gospel" contrary to that which they had received (Galatians 1:9). They had turned the biblical notion of justice into something it was never intended to be.

Lawlessness

But there is an equal and opposite error. It is what John Calvin called "antinomianism,"[7] what Martin Luther called "libertinism,"[8] and what Charles Spurgeon called "permissive and dismissive immorality."[9] The Bible calls it "worldliness" (1 Corinthians 3:3).

Like legalism, lawless disobedience is heresy. It is an attribute of rank ideological paganism and of the anti-Christ (2 Thessalonians 2:8). Although God loves righteousness, He hates lawlessness (Hebrews 1:9).

Jesus said:

> If anyone loves me, he will obey my teaching. My Father will love him, and we will come to him and make our home with him. He who does not love me will not obey my teaching. (John 14:23–24)

John MacArthur has asserted that this is "the Gospel according to Jesus,"[10] which is, he says, "a call to discipleship, a call to follow Him in submissive obedience, not just a plea to make a decision or say a prayer."[11] A life of faith, righteousness, holiness, and conse-cration will be demonstrable in both word and deed.

Any other message is, like legalism, "another" Gospel, a "differ-ent" Gospel, a "perverted" Gospel, an "accursed" Gospel (Galatians 1:6–9).

The Purpose of the Word

Christopher Morley once wrote that, "the enemies of the truth are always awfully nice."[12] The problem with both legalism and lawlessness is that they seem so nice, so well-intentioned—at least, at first glance. One brand or another of ideology seems to be as natural as breathing for us.

That is why we need an objective standard—one that stands

above even our experience. We need an absolute against which no encroachment of prejudice or preference may interfere. There must be a foundation that the winds of change and the waters of circumstance cannot erode. There must be a basis for truth and justice that can be depended upon at all times, in all places, and in every situation.

> There must be a basis for truth
> and justice that can be depended
> upon at all times, in all places,
> and in every situation.

The Bible is that standard, that absolute, and that foundation. All those who have gone before us in faith—patriarchs, prophets, apostles, preachers, evangelists, martyrs, and every righteous spirit made pure in Christ—have known that only too well.

The Bible is the Word of God. It reveals His wisdom, knowledge, understanding, and truth. It is not simply a splendid collection of inspiring sayings and stories. It is God's message to man. It is God's instruction. It is God's direction. It is God's guideline, His plumb-line, and His bottom-line.

From Genesis to Revelation the Bible is God's own Word. Nearly five thousand times throughout, the narrative is punctuated with phrases like "thus says the Lord," "thus the Lord commanded His people," or "thus came the Word of the Almighty."

Ultimately, only this "sure word" in the Bible—with all its uncomfortable offense—enables us to steer clear of the twin dangers of legalism and lawlessness.

Understand: We obey the Bible because we have been justified. We do not obey in order to be justified. Obedience to the Word is the effect of salvation, not the cause of salvation. In other words, daily submission to the statutes of God is a means of sanctification and transformation, not the means of justification and redemption. It is a way of life, not a way of salvation.

Jesus constantly upheld the validity of God's Word as a guide for living and an expression of the unchanging standards of His sovereign rule:

- It is easier for heaven and earth to pass away than for one stroke of a letter of the Law to fail (Luke 16:17).

- Anyone who breaks one of the least of these commandments and teaches others to do the same will be called least in the kingdom of heaven; but whoever practices and teaches these commands will be called great in the kingdom of heaven (Matthew 5:19).

Christ did not come to do away with the commands of God. On the contrary, He came to fulfill them—to confirm and uphold them (Matthew 5:17). He reiterated the fact that "the word of our God stands forever" (Isaiah 40:8).

Jesus was affirming that, unlike human lawmakers, God does not change His mind or alter His standards. When the Lord speaks, His Word stands firm forever. His assessments of right and wrong do not change from age to age.

Jesus appealed to God's eternal statutes to validate His teaching. He used them to vindicate His behavior. He used them to answer His questioners, to indict His opponents, to identify God's will, to establish kingdom citizenship, to confront Satan, and to confirm Christian love. He was, in short, a champion of the Word.[13]

True faith aims at God's satisfaction, while heresy aims at self-satisfaction.

But He also put the revelation of Scripture in its place. He showed us that obedience to the Word does not effect salvation for man. Instead, it is designed to effect holiness for men. It enables men and women to submit to the good providence of God in their lives.

This is what the apostle Paul meant when he said that we are no longer under the law, that in fact we are dead to the law. Instead, we come under the sacrificial covering of Christ's blood fulfilling the death sentence of the commandments against us. But the law is not thereby made void; rather, its curse is. In fact, when the commandments are put in their proper grace perspective, they are established.[14]

Far from being a replacement for grace, or being opposed to grace, the Bible teaches that the commandments and statutes are a provision of grace. "Is the law, therefore, opposed to the promises of God? Absolutely not!" (Galatians 3:21).

Manipulating God

The primary difference between biblical faith and heresy is that true religion is a response to truth and false religion attempts to manipulate God. True faith aims at God's satisfaction, while heresy aims at self-satisfaction.

Throughout the ages, men like Cain have used religion to get what they want. Men like Balaam have used religion to control circumstances. Men like Korah have used religion to enhance their position.[15] Cain, Balaam, and Korah all believed in the universal power of magic—either the magic of law or the magic of lawlessness. They believed that not only could they manipulate human society and natural elements with their peculiar approach to moral and ethical standards, but that God would also be forced to conform Himself to the desires and demands of men who act in terms of certain legal strictures: Say certain things, do certain things, believe certain things, or act out certain things, and God will have to respond. In essence, they believed that man controls his own destiny. They used either the rituals and formulas of legalism or the license and autonomy of lawlessness like magical talismans to attempt to save mankind, shape history, govern society, and even manipulate God.

Men continue to insist on rejecting the grace of God, and they have "taken the way of Cain; they have rushed for profit into Balaam's error; they have been destroyed in Korah's rebellion" (Jude 11).

That is why various forms of tyranny—from statism to anarchism—are so predominant among rebellious men and nations. By contrast, the great liberties that have been enjoyed in America over two hundred years of history were secured against the arbitrary and fickle whims of men and movements by the rule of law. American culture has not depended upon the benevolence of the magistrates, or the altruism of the wealthy, or the condescension of the powerful. Every citizen, rich or poor, man or woman, native-born or immigrant, hale or handicapped, young or old, has been considered equal under the standard of unchanging, immutable, and impartial justice.

As Thomas Paine wrote in *Common Sense*, the powerful booklet that helped spark the War for Independence, "In America, the law is king."[16]

If left to the mere discretion of human authorities, all statutes, edicts, and ordinances inevitably devolve into tyranny. There must be a dependable and unchanging basis for justice—and the only firm basis is biblical righteousness.

Apart from this uniquely Christian innovation in the affairs of men there can be no hope of freedom or justice. There never has been before, and there never will be again. Many of our republic's founding fathers knew that well.

The opening refrain of the Declaration of Independence, for instance, affirms the necessity of an absolute standard upon which justice is derived:

> We hold these truths to be self-evident, that all men are created equal; that they are endowed by their Creator with certain inalienable rights; that among these are life, liberty, and the pursuit of happiness. That, to secure these rights, governments are instituted among men, deriving their just powers from the consent of the governed.[17]

The framers committed themselves and their posterity to the absolute standard of "the laws of nature and nature's God."[18] And the essence of that standard, they said, were certain "inalienable," "universal," "God-given," and sovereignly "endowed" rights. Take the scriptural standard away, and no standard of justice is possible.

Sadly, this has been thrown into very real jeopardy in our day— in all our human relations, in and out of the church. No one is absolutely secure, because absoluteness has been thrown out of our operational vocabularies. All the liberties and all the protections of all people are at risk because suddenly arbitrariness, relativism, and randomness have entered the legal, cultural, and spiritual equations. The checks against petty partiality and blatant bias have been forcibly disabled.

Just as they had been in Christ's time by the Pharisees and Herodians.

Strange Bedfellows

The Pharisees in ancient Israel were a party of religious legalists. The Herodians were a party of lawless secularists. The Pharisees' name literally meant "the separatists," because they were so concerned to remain unstained by the world. The Herodians' name implied a close connection with one of the most worldly, vile, and xenophobic men in all history. The Pharisees withdrew from occupations of power and influence in order to focus on "spiritual things." The Herodians grasped for such occupations with undeterred zeal in order to focus on "earthly things."

And yet these two parties, so diametrically opposed in every other way, became partners by their opposition to Jesus (Mark 3:6). Paganism makes for strange bedfellows.

The Pharisees opposed Jesus because they felt He had polluted the spiritual realm with earthly cares—such as caring for the poor. The Herodians opposed Jesus because they felt He had polluted the earthly realm with spiritual cares—such as bringing every area of life publicly under the province of God's rule.

So the two parties—the legalistic escapists and the lawless materialists—became co-belligerants. They joined forces to assert a separation between faith and culture, between religion and activism, between righteousness and justice—much like the modern division between church and state. They joined together in opposition to the Gospel of Christ and its biblical balance.

The party of the Pharisees emphasized a separatist view of piety wherein a sharp division is made between the "spiritual" and the "material." They considered the "spiritual" realm to be superior to the "material." All things physical, all things temporal, all things earthly were spurned. The cultural apparatus was thus left in the hands of evildoers.

Meanwhile, the party of the Herodians was busy with its work of oppression and repression. The Herodians held seats of cultural power: in government, in education, in the judiciary, and in the financial world. They cared nothing for the morality of the Pharisees. They abhorred the Pharisees' puritanical legalism. They chafed against their piety. They despised their nonconformity.

But, they applauded their irrelevancy. They appreciated their distraction from the things of this world. They knew that as long as the Pharisees maintained a clear separation between justice and righteousness, the Herodians would continue to have a free rein. They would be able to perpetuate their defamation of all things holy, all things sacred, and all things pure.

In this paradoxical fashion, the Herodians counted the irrelevant, isolationist Pharisees as their most trusted allies. And vice versa.

Betwixt and Between

He was America's first celebrity. Though just twenty-five years old when he began touring the sparsely settled colonies in 1738, George Whitefield was an immediate sensation. And he remained so for the rest of his life. Over the next thirty years, amidst seven visits from his native England, he would leave his mark on the lives of virtually every English-speaking soul living on this side of the Atlantic—from the cosmopolitan businessmen of Philadelphia and the seasoned traders of Boston to the farmers of Virginia and the frontier adventurers of Canada.

He took America by storm. "When he arrived in the colonies," says historian Mark Noll, "he was simply an event."[19] Wherever he went, vast crowds gathered to hear him. Commerce ceased. Shops closed. Farmers left their plows mid-furrow. And affairs of the greatest import were postponed. One of his sermons in the Boston Common actually drew more listeners than the city's entire population. Another in Philadelphia spilled over onto more than a dozen city blocks. Still another in Savannah recorded the largest single crowd ever to gather anywhere in the colonies—despite the scant local population.

By all accounts, he was the "father of modern evangelism."[20] He sparked a revival of portentous proportions—the Great Awakening.[21] He pioneered one of the most enduring church reform movements—Methodism.[22] And he laid the foundations for perhaps the greatest experiment in liberty the world has yet known—the American Republic.[23]

All the greatest men of the day were in unabashed awe of his oratorical prowess. Shakespearean actor David Garrick said, "I would give a hundred guineas if I could say *oh* like Mr. Whitefield."[24] Benjamin Franklin once quipped, "He can bring men to tears merely by pronouncing the word *Mesopotamia*."[25]

But he was equally beloved for his righteous character. George Washington said, "Upon his lips the Gospel appears even to the coarsest of men as sweet and as true as, in fact, it is."[26] Patrick Henry mused, "Would that every bearer of God's glad tidings be as fit a vessel of grace as Mr. Whitefield."[27] And the poet, John Greenleaf Whittier wrote of him:

> That life of pure intent,That voice of warning, yet eloquent, Of one on the errands of angels sent.[28]

Yet despite his wide acclaim and popularity, Whitefield was often ridiculed, scorned, and persecuted for his faith. Hecklers blew trumpets and shouted obscenities at him as he preached. Enraged mobs often attacked his meetings, robbing, beating, and humiliating his followers. Men were maimed. Women were stripped and occasionally raped. Whitefield himself was subjected to unimaginable brutality—he was clubbed twice, stoned once, whipped at least half a dozen times, and beaten a half a dozen more. And he lived constantly under the pall of death threats. Once, he recorded in his journal: "I was honored with having a few stones, dirt, rotten eggs, and pieces of dead cats thrown at me. Nevertheless, the Lord was gracious, and a great number were awakened unto life."[29]

Amazingly, it was not just the profane who condemned Whitefield's work. He was also opposed by the religious establishment. Accused of being a fanatic and of being intolerant, he was often in "more danger of attack from the clergy than he was from the worldly."[30]

Yet he fearlessly faced his opposition and continued his work. Though often stung by the vehemence of the opposition he faced, he refused to take it personally, attributing it rather to the "offense of the Gospel."[31]

According to J. I. Packer, most of the English-speaking Christians in Whitefield's day "had taken up with a moralistic, indeed legalistic, recasting of justification by faith."[32]

Whitefield believed that this sort of faith was not only "destructive nonsense," it was actually "blasphemous." It was, he believed, "the religion of the natural man masquerading as Christianity" and was thus "the most common evil that was ever under the sun." It produced "a religion of aspiration, perspiration, and in sensitive souls, periodic desperation."[33]

Nevertheless, such a religion was popular and accepted. It always is.

Thus, despite the fact that Whitefield struck a sensitive chord and won a wide following among the people when he proclaimed the old Puritan doctrines of grace, he also stirred up fierce opposition among both the ungodly and the religious—who always have been, and always will be, united in their animosity toward the Gospel.

Whitefield emphasized that a comprehension of grace would prompt wholehearted righteousness—thus there was actually no contradiction between the requisites of Christian holiness and the prerogatives of Christian liberty. And that was equally an offense to the person who desired no accountability to a moral standard whatsoever and the person who desired to reduce the faith to a series of moral demands. To both the lawless and the legalist, Whitefield's message of life in Christ was intolerable.

It still is.

Taking the Offensive

It seems that the balanced message of the prophet Micah was offensive to the people of his day. To some it smacked of overly-spiritualized judgment. To others it seemed too worldly-minded and secular. To all of them it was an unwelcome interruption of the status quo. It was an uncomfortable reminder that neither an obsession with the world that embraces the domination of evil nor a neglect of the world that concedes the domination of evil is acceptable in the sight of the Lord.

Eadburgh of Bicester, a princess of Mercia in seventh-century England known for her holy life and good deeds among the poor of Aylesbury, underscored the importance of fulfilling the Micah Mandate in the face of such tragic ironies:

> We do the lost and lonely, the desperate and deprived no favors by offering them anything less than the offense of the Gospel. There is no tenderness of heart, no sensitivity of soul, no generosity of spirit in accommodating men's sin in this life when the consequences be so dire in the next. Let us therefore hold firmly to this

just cause, let us therefore raise up this just banner: His Word alone. In this fashion do we fulfill what the Lord requires: but to do justly.[34]

That may not appear to be either fish or fowl to the ideological minions of this poor fallen world—but it is right and good and true. And, it is just.

JUST DESSERTS

"He has showed you, O man, what is good. And what does the Lord require of you? To act justly and to love mercy and to walk humbly with your God"
(Micah 6:8).

True justice, being a faithful adherence to God's Word as opposed to some worldly ideological system, has always been a passion for the heroes of the faith through the ages. Despite the conspiratorial scorn of both legalists and those who wanted to live without rules, they stood their ground and brought their every deed in focus with the Gospel. Examples abound:

Thomas of Villanueva (1488–1535) grew up in the region of Don Quixote's La Mancha in a devout Christian home where virtuous living and charity were constantly modeled for him by his parents. It was no surprise then when he committed himself to a life of Christian service after graduating from the new university at Alcala. In 1518, at the age of thirty, he was ordained and began a career as an anointed and effective preacher. His ministry was most distinguished not by his pulpit skills, however, but rather by his care and concern for the poor and needy. He was especially involved in providing relief for abused children and orphans—securing new homes for them as well as meeting their immediate material needs. He was involved in other pro-life activities as well: Once, when he discovered an abortion cabal operating illicitly in a nearby city, he flew into a frenzy of righteous indignation—provoking a criminal investigation and eliciting stronger laws for the protection of children. Relying on neither legalism nor lawlessness, he raised the standard of justice in the land.

A sudden and glorious conversion transformed *Camillus de Lellis* (1555–89) from a gruff soldier of fortune into a meek and compassionate servant of Christ. Because he himself had suffered from a chronic affliction, shortly after his decision to trust the Lord he offered himself to the hospital of San Giacomo in Rome, of which he quickly became bursar. This experience opened his eyes to the shocking brutalities of Renaissance life. He began to train and supervise teams of Christian workers, not only to care for the sick but to deal with some of the entrenched problems of the poor, the homeless, and the abandoned that led to disease and contagion. Before the end of the sixteenth century, he had established several hospitals and hospices in Naples to handle the second- and third-order consequences of both legalism and lawlessness, becoming a champion of justice for thousands.

Education was the privilege of the very few and the very rich until *Jean Baptist De La Salle* (1621–88) began his great work midway through the seventeenth century. After giving up a life of ease, he dedicated himself to teaching the children of the very poor. He opened day schools, Sunday schools, vocational training schools, teachers' colleges, and continuing education centers— actually pioneering many modern techniques and concepts—in more than fourteen cities throughout Europe. He fought hard against the insipid humanistic tendencies within the scholastic community, and he deplored the corresponding decline in Christian morality. He believed that if youngsters could be educated in accordance with Gospel principles, the barbarities of both legalism and lawlessness would disappear; but if they were not given the opportunity to advance, such wickedness would eventually prevail—because, as he often said, evil desires nothing better than hopelessness and ignorance.

Dozens of others could be cited throughout the wide span of history: Gregory the Great (d. 604) Margaret of Scotland (d. 1093), Sava of Trnova (d. 1235), Bonaventure of Bagnorea (d. 1286), Seriphim of Sarov (d. 1833), William Carey (d. 1834), and Jai Ishii of

Okayama (d. 1899). Each took the Scriptures as their byword for everything in life. And thus, they left us a legacy of justice unparalleled in all of human history.

TRUTH, JUSTICE, AND THE AMERICAN WAY

"He has showed you, O man, what is good.
And what does the Lord require of you? To act
justly and to love mercy and to walk humbly
with your God" (Micah 6:8).

Our conception of justice is so dominated by modern ideological categories that it is often difficult to see it in any other light. Why not make a conscious effort to redefine the concept from a biblical perspective—entirely free of liberal or conservative proof texts or notions. Follow the word "justice" through the Scriptures to see how it is used. Particularly notice how Micah's contemporaries, Isaiah and Hosea, use it in their prophecies.

During the Reformation and then later during the American Revolution, the subject of justice was often addressed in sermons, tracts, and Christian books. Take some time to go to a library and read through some of these great works of the past to see how your vision of justice stacks up against those who have gone before us in faith. See particularly the wonderful anthology edited by Ellis Sandoz entitled *Sermons of the American Founding Era,* published by Liberty Press.

Justice is something that we do, not just something that we believe in. Are you aware of injustices that need to be rectified in your community? Is there something that you can do? Is there something that you ought to do? Well, what are you waiting for?

Notes

1. George Grant, *The 57% Solution* (Franklin, Tenn.: Adroit Press, 1993), 60.

2. Horton Kael and William Loomis, *A Documentary History of Liberal Thought* (New York: M. H. Cushman, 1956), 246.

3. Ibid., 228.

4. Ibid.

5. Isaiah 1:10–18; Amos 5:1–7; Habakkuk 2:4; Psalm 32:1–2; Psalm 51:1–17; Galatians 3:10–11; Ephesians 2:8–9; John 15:4–6; Jude 20–21; 2 Peter 1:3–4.

6. Galatians 5:11; Galatians 2:21; Galatians 3:3–5; Romans 4:4.

7. Bernard Laslo, *A Christian's Holiness* (London: Gospel Colporterage Society, 1929), 19.

8. Ibid.

9. Ibid.

10. John MacArthur, *The Gospel According to Jesus* (Grand Rapids: Zondervan, 1988), 21.

11. Ibid.

12. William Dougherty, *Animosity Toward the Future* (New York: Carson and Lowe, 1981), 246.

13. John 8:17; Matthew 12:5; Luke 10:26; John 7:19; Matthew 19:17; Matthew 7:24; Matthew 4:1–11; John 14:21.

14. Romans 6:14–15; Romans 7:4; Galatians 2:19; Romans 8:1–2; Galatians 3:13; Romans 3:31.

15. Cain—Genesis 4:3–8; Hebrews 11:4; 1 John 3:12; Balaam—Numbers 31:16; 2 Peter 2:15; Revelation 2:14; Korah—Numbers 16:1–3; 31–35.

16. Thomas Paine, *Common Sense* (New York: Bartlet and Caine, 1991), 14.

17. Karl Temple, ed., *Documentary History of America* (New York: Thompson and Evans, 1977), 33.

18. Ibid.

19. *Christian History*, XII: 2.

20. Although there were a great many innovative evangelists both before and after Whitefield who contributed to modern evangelistic methodology and practice, Whitefield stands out in innumerable ways. See J. C. Ryle, *Christian Leaders of the Eighteenth Century* (Edinburgh, U.K.: Banner of Truth Trust, 1978).

21. Again, a great number of notables contributed to the flowering of the Great Awakening. But none more significantly than Whitefield. See John Pollock, *George Whitefield and the Great Awakening* (Tring, U.K.: Lion, 1972).

22. Though John and Charles Wesley are today known as the founders of Methodism, it was Whitefield who actually enticed them to join his fledgling movement. See Arnold Dallimore, *George Whitefield* (Wheaton, Ill.: Crossway, 1990).

23. The connection between the ideas of Christian liberty exposited by Whitefield and the ideas of political liberty expounded by the founding fathers has been ably explored in numerous scholarly works. See Ellis Sandoz, *Political Sermons of the American Founding Era* (Indianapolis: Liberty, 1991).

24. Carl Vrestead, *Whitefield* (London: Empire Bible Association, 1936), 44.

25. Ibid.

26. Ibid., 45.

27. Ibid.

28. Ibid.

29. Ibid., 90.

30. Ibid.

31. Vrestead, 91.

32. Christian History, XII: 2.

33. Ibid.

34. *Oxford Archeological Society*, LXXX: 44.

GOOD NEWS V. NICE NEWS

That it does not matter what a man believes is a statement heard on every side today. The statement carries a fearful implication. The statement really means that it does not matter what a man believes so long as he does not take his beliefs seriously.
Richard Weaver

It was late and I was tired. I had spoken five times that day at a large pro-life conference in Houston. My back ached, my throat was sore, the shower wasn't working properly in my hotel room, and I desperately missed my family. So, I decided to skip dinner and curl up with a good medieval mystery before turning in for the night. I was just getting comfortable when the phone rang.

A local pastor, Ben Jackson, had attended the conference and was now full of questions. He wanted to know if I had some time to talk. I was about to tell him that I just couldn't when he mentioned that he thought that we might want to step out for a barbecue brisket sandwich.

I have a particular weakness for barbecue. I've had shredded pork in Knoxville, pit-roast in Richmond, honey-back in Charlotte, pollo loco in Miami, yankee links in New York, and charred cabritto in Santa Fe. I've even sampled Chen's Mongolian barbecue in London and Ferrot's Canadian ribs in Ottawa. But my favorite—by far—is Texas-style brisket.

Needless to say, I was sufficiently enticed to abandon my plans for a quiet evening.

Ben picked me up downstairs in the hotel lobby, and we drove across the vast surreal suburban landscape that dominates the area just north of the city. What was little more than an uninhabited stretch of piney woods two decades ago is now a continuous sprawl of strip shopping centers, apartment complexes, and upper-middle-class bedroom communities. Finally we stopped at Luther's—a Texas barbecue tradition aggressively franchised throughout the region.

As we found a quiet table in a corner of the barn-like restaurant, Ben told me that he had been pastoring for more than fifteen years. And everywhere he had served during those years, he had met with great success. His current church had grown from just under a hundred to more than seven hundred members during the past three years. He had undertaken two ambitious building pro-grams, added three new staff members, and started a small mission project—all without incurring any long-term debt. He hosted a popular daily radio broadcast, he was recently elected chairman of the local ministers' alliance, he had been asked to serve on the board of an independent community hospital, and he was widely respected throughout the entire metropolitan area. He had an ideal home life—with a beautiful and talented wife and four "per-fect" young children.

I kept waiting for the inevitable "but. . . ." He was the picture of prosperity and achievement. Nevertheless, it was obvious that he was supremely dissatisfied.

He went on to tell me that he felt trapped by the very success he had worked so hard for. He no longer felt like he could say what he needed to say, do what he needed to do. There was now too much at stake. He had too much to lose.

"Sometimes I feel as if I'm caught in a vise-grip of propriety. I know that I have an obligation to equip and inform the members of our church to deal with the grave problems of our culture, but to even raise those issues is offensive to many of them. They just immediately react. And that jeopardizes everything else that we're trying to do."

He explained to me his attempts over the last year or so to gen-tly nudge the church toward involvement in any one of a number of projects—ranging from pro-life awareness to concern over pornography—all to no avail. The previous January, on the anniversary of Roe v. Wade, he preached from a very familiar text:

"The just shall live by faith" (Romans 1:17 KJV).

"I said that though this verse was normally understood as an exhortation for believers to walk in faith, the apostle Paul makes it clear that the faithful believer was also to be *just*. I then dealt with the whole issue of biblical justice and tried to apply it to the questions of abortion-on-demand and the runaway liberal activism of the courts."

Needless to say, the sermon did not go over well with some of the folks who sat in the pews that morning. Ben was scolded by a handful of prominent members for getting "too political" from the pulpit. Several elders and deacons asked him to "tone it down" in the future. A few people even threatened to leave the church.

"They said my message was offensive. That I was bordering on intolerance. That I shouldn't deal with such complex issues as justice. That I should just stick with the Gospel and leave out all the controversial stuff."

Ben wanted to know how to deal with the tough issues of our day without alienating people. He wanted a formula for continued success that would enable him to deal with offensive questions without being offensive.

"I think I'm pretty representative of a lot of people in the church today—whether they're in leadership or not. I don't want to run off the very people that I've tried so long to attract. I don't want to be judgmental, condemning, or closed-minded. We live in a pluralistic society, after all. Times have changed."

I knew the struggle that Ben was going through. We all want to be liked. We all want to be winsome. We want to present the world with a message that is attractive, uplifting, and cheery. We want to come across as friendly. We want to be nice. But the fact is that whenever we try to stand up for right against wrong, whenever we attempt to defend truth against deception, whenever we champion justice in the face of injustice, we're likely to ruffle some feathers. It can't be avoided.

The words "justice" and "judgment" are actually used interchangeably throughout the Bible. And for good reason. What is right and just and true contradicts and condemns what is evil and wicked and perverse. And that is bound to be offensive to some people.

There was a long pause in our conversation. The jukebox was

wailing a sad country song and the barbecue was getting cold. Finally, he said, "I'm not sure that it's possible to be both successful and faithful in America today."

"I guess it all just depends on how you define those terms," I replied.

> It matters not who we may be or
> from whence we come, the
> Gospel is an affront to all that we
> have done and to all that we are.

Taking Offense

The renowned Welsh preacher of the last generation, D. Martyn Lloyd-Jones, once remarked, "The great effect of our Lord's preaching was to make everybody feel condemned, and nobody likes that."[1]

On almost every page of the New Testament, we find Jesus offending someone. When He wasn't confronting the Scribes and the Pharisees, He was rebuking the promiscuous and the perverse. When He wasn't alienating the Sadducees and the Herodians, He was reproving the tax-collectors and the prostitutes. He even had a knack for estranging His own disciples with His "hard teachings" (John 6:60).

Jesus "meek and mild" was rarely meek or mild when it came to sin. He pulled no punches. Philosopher and theologian Michael Bauman has commented:

> At various times, and when the situation demanded, Jesus pub-
> licly denounced sinners as snakes, dogs, foxes, hypocrites, fouled
> tombs, and dirty dishes. He actually referred to one of His chief
> disciples as Satan. So that His hearers would not miss the point,
> He sometimes referred to the objects of his most intense ridicule
> both by name and by position, and often face to face. . . . He well
> understood that sometimes it is wrong to be nice.[2]

He was an equal-opportunity offender.

Christ came into this world to call all humanity unto repentance. Thus His message stands out as an unflinching condemnation of the fallen estate of all humanity: the great and the small, the good and the bad, the weak and the strong, the rich and the poor. It matters not who we may be or from whence we come, the Gospel is an affront to all that we have done and to all that we are:

> There is none righteous, not even one; there is no one who under-
> stands, no one who seeks God. All have turned away, they have
> together become worthless; there is no one who does good, not
> even one. (Romans 3:10–12)

Such a message was never intended to be popular; it was intend-ed to be true. We all desperately need Good News, not nice news.

And that is simply not a popular notion. Not now. Not ever. Thus, "He came unto that which was his own, but his own did not receive him" (John 1:11).

Church-growth experts tell us that controversial or confronta-tional preaching will do more to drive people away than to draw them in. They tell us that sermons ought to appeal to the lowest-common-denominator, that services ought to be simple and acces-sible, and that programs ought to be consumer-oriented and user-friendly—otherwise we may offend rather than attract. They tell us that substantive theology will at best confuse the average churchgoer, and at worst, alienate him.

And, they're probably right—as the ministry of Jesus amply demonstrates. His insistence that the demands of justice ultimately had to be satisfied was an affront to virtually everyone who heard Him.

It still is.

The unvarnished truth is just as offensive to us as it was to Christ's contemporaries. We don't want to hear that our hearts are "deceitful above all things and beyond cure" (Jeremiah 17:9). We don't want to hear that we have all sinned and fallen short of the glory of God or that the wages of sin is death. We don't want to hear that our corrupt lives have resulted in a corrupt culture where the innocent are exploited, the helpless are despoiled, and the downtrodden are forgotten. We don't want to hear that there are very real and tangible consequences to our sin that ultimately must be dealt with. We would much rather find a series of steps that would "enable" us, "empower" us, or help us to "recover," than we would to hear the clear message of grace.

As a result, "It is often our moral duty," says Oswald Chambers, "to give offense."[3]

And offense is easy enough to give. All we have to do is to say what the Bible says. All we have to teach is what the Bible teaches. We don't have to launch a crusade or provoke a revolution. We need not lower ourselves to rudeness, crudeness, or a lack of sophistication. The Bible is enough to send the purveyors of politically-correct multi-cultural bibblebabble into absolute conniptions. The scriptural message of justice, mercy, and humble faith is "foolishness" to some. It is a "stumbling block" to others. But it is an "offense" to all who disbelieve.

That is why people can't be ambivalent about biblical justice. That is why they have to react so violently to its demands. That is why they are able to be so tolerant of anything and everything except the call to affirm biblical standards of justice in our lives and in our communities. And that is why they are so intent on erecting new guidelines for an orthodoxy of their own making—a compromised hodgepodge of that "anything and everything" called "pluralism."

Pluralism

Pluralism has always been hard to define. Its topsy-turvy logic is often as unintelligible as medieval runes. In practice, it is an odd attempt to forge a cultural consensus on the idea that there can be no cultural consensus. It is the unspoken assumption that a happy and harmonious society can be maintained only so long as the only common belief is that there are no common beliefs. It is the reluctant affirmation that the only absolute is that there must not be any absolutes.

"Why can't we all just get along?" is the mantra of pluralism. Don't condemn anyone. Don't judge others. Respect diversity. Different strokes for different folks.

The advocates of pluralism claim that there is something more on a community level to the notion than this kind of blind toleration and diversity, of course. Walter Lippmann called this "something more" the "public philosophy,"[4] and James Madison called it the "public good."[5]

According to Os Guinness, many things are included in this "mostly unwritten" and "often half-conscious" sort of "common vision." Those things range from "shared ideals, such as honesty and loyalty" to "shared understandings, such as the relationship of religion and public life."[6]

But that is just so much wishful thinking. We no longer share the ideals of honesty and loyalty—if we ever did. And we certainly don't agree about the place of religion in public life—just ask the ACLU. To pretend otherwise is worse than naïveté. It is willful denial.

> # What can be a legitimate law if our ultimate values have to be continuously updated by sifting them through the filter of popular opinion and the will of the 51 percent?

Our society has lost whatever ethical cohesion we once had. And as a result we are embroiled in an intractable conflict—what James Dobson has dubbed the "civil war of values"[7] and what James Davison Hunter has called the "culture war."[8]

Who decides what is and what is not a part of pluralism's "common vision"? Who defines just what "honesty" entails? Or "loyalty"? Or any other "ideal," for that matter? At what point does "diversity" become "fragmentation"?

And what is justice? What can be a legitimate law if our ultimate values have to be continuously updated by sifting them through the filter of popular opinion and the will of the 51 percent? Is the public-opinion poll our only source of the voice of virtue?

The advocates of radical pluralism have yet to supply good answers to such dilemmas. Nevertheless, pluralism is now the assumed basis for American culture and life.

It ought to be obvious that any society that has ceased to hold in common certain essential assumptions about life and morals cannot long survive. A hazy pluralism—with its lowered standards, diluted ethics, and compromised integrity—is not only insufficient to hold a society together, it actually militates against the very possibility of cohesion. Justice is necessarily tossed to and fro on waves of doubt. Truth changes from one day to the next. Anarchy or tyranny actually becomes the best of a host of other undesirable options.

It is just as absurd to say that any idea is as valid as every idea, as it is to say that bad ideas are as helpful as good ideas. It is equally ridiculous to say that there is no difference between right and wrong as it is to say that there is no difference between right and left. We have somehow failed to grasp the fact that too many moralities and not enough morals will result in chaos.

By drenching the notion of pluralism in what C. S. Lewis called "a perpetual lukewarm shower bath of sentimentality"[9] we have obscured its disastrous illogic. But no amount of rhetorical pleasantries about unity in diversity can obscure its results.

Hell on Earth

An avalanche of perversity has crashed over our land in recent years, laying waste nearly everything in its path. A veritable Pandora's Box of evils has been unleashed by the champions and purveyors of pluralism. Thus, rampant immorality has begun to significantly erode the stability of our cultural foundations.

Pornography has become a frighteningly powerful multi-billion-dollar-a-year industry in the U.S. and Canada—with higher sales figures than even McDonald's.[10] It has, in fact, become the fastest growing segment of the American "entertainment" industry.[11] With its very clear connections with violent crime, organized crime, and societal dysfunction, all the various manifestations of pornography—soft porn, hard porn, child porn, violent porn, live porn, video porn, phone porn, cable porn, peep porn, and snuff porn—are dangerous incursions on the security and liberty of us all.[12]

Prostitution, like pornography, is becoming an ever more dominant factor in the economics of our nation.[13] With the proliferation of bath houses, massage parlors, escort services, nude bars, and swank bordellos in virtually every region, the once seedy and shadowy profession has been transformed into a far-flung multi-million-dollar-a-year modern industry—in many places legal, in most others, entirely unregulated.[14]

Promiscuity now runs rampant. The "sexual revolution" has come and gone, leaving in its wake innumerable casualties—as all revolutions are wont to do. Recent studies indicate that the residual damage is even worse than what we might expect.[15] Only 31 percent of American women wait until marriage before engaging in sexual relations. Only 20 percent of men do. Forty-three percent of teens under the age of seventeen have already initiated sexual activity.[16]

It is now difficult to keep track of the vast array of publicly-endorsed and institutionally-supported sexual aberrations. And the rate of infection from a variety of sexually transmitted diseases—from syphilis and herpes to gonorrhea and AIDS—has reached epidemic proportions.

Add to this litany of woes the abortion holocaust, the rapid encroachments of euthanasia, and the dramatic increase in drug abuse, and you have all the ingredients for complete cultural disaster.

> What moral standard should we
> use when we legislate? Will it be the
> unchanging, unerring scriptural
> prescription for justice, or will
> it be the ever-shifting notion
> of pluralistic accommodation?

In a pluralistic society, each of these woes falls into the gray and hazy domain of "victimless crimes"—in other words, no one is involved or harmed except "consenting adults." And so, they fall beyond the reach of justice. Advocates of pluralism maintain—in both their literature and in the innumerable court cases they have undertaken—that such issues should stand entirely outside the concern of the community or the citizenry.[17] They argue that to impose any "community standards" of ethics and decency is "a violation of the spirit of American democracy" and a "contradiction of our most basic constitutional tenets."[18] Any attempt to do so is instantly dubbed "intolerance," "bigotry," "zealotry and insensitivity," or "the excesses of religious fundamentalism."

Amazingly, the vast proportion of the modern church has accepted this notion—if not in principle, then in practice. We shy away from the biblical imperative to "act justly and to love mercy and to walk humbly" with our God (Micah 6:8). We don't want to get sidetracked by peripheral issues that might deflect interest in the Gospel. We don't want to offend anyone.

"And besides," we reason, "you can't legislate morality in a pluralistic society."

Legislating Morality

On the contrary, as D. James Kennedy has so often asserted, "Morality is the only thing you *can* legislate."[19] That's what legislation is—the codification in law of some particular moral concern—generally so that the immorality of a few is not forcibly inflicted on the rest of us. Legislating morality is the very cornerstone of justice.

Murder is against the law because we recognize that the premeditated killing of another human being is a violation of a very basic and fundamental moral principle: the sanctity of human life. Theft is against the law because we recognize that taking someone else's belongings without permission is a breach of another one of our most basic and fundamental ethical standards: the inviolability of private property. The fact is, all law is some moral or ethical tenet raised up to social enforceability by the civil sphere. Thus, the question is not "*Should* we legislate morality?" Rather, it is "*Whose* morality should we legislate?" The question is, "*What* moral standard should we use when we legislate?" Will it be the unchanging, unerring scriptural prescription for justice, or will it be the ever-shifting notion of pluralistic accommodation?

The fact is, genuine pluralism is a practical impossibility. A brash and cavalier attitude toward any exclusive standard of goodness and morality is perhaps the single most distressing trait of modern pluralism. In the name of civil liberties, cultural diversity, and political-correctness, American culture has pressed forward a radical agenda of willy-nilly moral corruption and ethical degeneration.

Ironically, its brazen disregard for any objective standard of decency and its defense of perverse behavior has threatened our liberties and diversity because it has threatened the foundations that made those things possible in the first place.

Pluralism wants the privileges of America bestowed upon the citizenry as an unearned, undeserved, and unwarranted entitlement. Apart from the grace of God, though, there simply cannot be any such entitlement in human societies. Great privileges bring with them great responsibilities. Our remarkable freedom has been bought with a price. And that price was moral diligence, virtuous sacrifice, and ethical uprightness. The legal commitment of pluralism to any and all of the fanatically twisted fringes of American culture—pornographers, gay activists, abortionists, and other professional liberationists—is a self-defeating crusade that has confused liberty with license.

Aleksandr Solzhenitsyn, the brilliant Russian novelist, historian, and Nobel laureate, has said:

> Fifty years ago it would have seemed quite impossible in America that an individual be granted boundless freedom with no purpose but simply for the satisfaction of his whims. The defense of individual rights has reached such extremes as to make society as a whole defenseless. It is time to defend, not so much human rights, as human obligations.[20]

According to James Q. Wilson, pluralism's terms are misleading:

> Many people have persuaded themselves that children will be harmed if they are told right from wrong; instead they should be encouraged to discuss the merits of moral alternatives. This is called *values clarification*, but I think it a recipe for confusion rather than clarity. Many people have persuaded themselves that it is wrong to judge the customs of another society since there are no standards apart from custom on which such judgments can rest; presumably they would oppose infanticide only if it involved their own child. This is sometimes called *tolerance;* I think a better name would be barbarism.[21]

Practical experience weighs heavily against the possibility of pluralism. But perhaps the strongest argument against pluralism is the simplest: It is the existence of hell.

It is not sound logic, politics, legal systems, cultural preference, economic feasibility, or even necessity that makes the pipe-dreams of pluralism so fabulous. It is the fact that God will one day judge all men. It is the fact that His judgment is unqualified and final. It is that the demands of justice ultimately must be satisfied.

It does not matter what people believe or what they do only if what they believe and what they do actually does not matter. But hell offers vivid testimony that it does indeed matter. Moral absolutes matter. Ethical standards matter. Virtue and vice matter. Right and wrong matter. Good and bad matter. Justice and injustice matter. They matter because the eternal destiny of men hangs upon their determination.

The entire witness of Western civilization bears this out. Thus, through the ages faithful men have boldly cut across the grain of comfort and convention, warning sinners of their dire danger.

Hellfire and Brimstone

Unlike his friend George Whitefield, Jonathan Edwards was not a particularly enthralling master of pulpit theatrics or hermeneutics. Instead, he won his reputation as a thinker. He was highly regarded as a "precise dogmatician" and a "careful systemizer."[22]

As a philosopher, his greatness was unmatched.

Benjamin Franklin said that he "had a rational mind unmatched for generations untold."[23] Daniel Webster said that his books were among the "greatest achievements of the human intellect."[24]

But as a preacher, he apparently left a little something to be desired.

In fact, he read his densely theological and philosophical sermons from longhand manuscripts—often in a flat, monotonous voice. Only rarely did he make eye contact with his congregation. Though not unpleasant in demeanor, he hardly cut a dashing or charismatic figure.

A member of his church described these deficiencies sympathetically:

> His appearance in the pulpit was with a good grace, and his delivery easy, natural, but very solemn. He had not a strong voice but appeared with such gravity, and spake with such distinctness and precision—his words so full of ideas and set in such a plain and striking light—that few speakers have been so able to demand the attention of an audience as he. His words often discovered a great degree of inward fervor, without much noise or external emotion, and fell with great weight on the minds of his hearers. He made

but little motion of his head or hands in the pulpit, but spake as to discover the motion of his own heart, which tended in the most natural and effectual manner to move and affect others.[25]

But another said:

I can little explain how the assembly remains awake during his discourses—which are over-long, boorish, and often incomprehensible to the simple man. Though there is evidence of some great passion in thought, yet to the eye and ear, little or none.[26]

Nevertheless, on July 8, 1741, Edwards traveled a few miles from his home into western Connecticut and read to a small congregation assembled there America's most famous sermon.

Entitled *Sinners in the Hands of an Angry God*, the sermon was an exposition of the text, "Their foot shall slide in due time" (Deuteronomy 32:35 KJV). Its subject was the imminence of judgment and the horrors of perdition.

The sermon was terrifyingly vivid:

Yea, God is a great deal more angry with great numbers that are now on the earth; yea doubtless, with many that are now in this congregation, who it may be are at ease, than He is with many of those who are now in the flames of Hell. The wrath of God burns against them, their damnation does not slumber; the pit is prepared, the fire is made ready; the furnace is now hot ready to receive them; the flames do now rage and glow; the glittering sword is now whet and held over them. Unconverted men walk over the pit of Hell on a rotten covering, and there are innumerable places in this covering so weak that they will not bear their own weight, and these places are not seen.[27]

The sermon caused an immediate sensation in the town of Enfield where it was preached. According to historian John Currid, even before the sermon was finished, "people were moaning, groaning and crying out" such things as "What shall I do to be saved?"[28] In fact, there was such a "breathing of distress and weeping" that Edwards had to quiet and calm the people several times so he could conclude. The fervor of the Great Awakening that had thus far bypassed Enfield now swept through the little town with a white-hot intensity. Suddenly the people were convicted of sin. The Holy Spirit empowered his preaching to such an extent that a revival was inevitable.

In short order, the sermon was printed and widely distributed throughout the Americas. It not only won for Edwards even greater renown than he already enjoyed, but it provoked a further awakening among its distant readers. Since then it has been reprinted hundreds of times—perhaps thousands. To this day it is not only a standard text for the study of great preaching, it has passed into the realm of classic literature—and thus is the most anthologized sermon in the English language.

Though obviously anointed with divine favor, *Sinners in the Hands of an Angry God*—like so much of the rest of his vast body of work—was not without controversy. Many said that Edwards illegitimately played upon people's emotions. Others said that he shamelessly exploited the popular fears and phobias of the day.[29]

The Good News is that the bad news is bad— and yet hope remains.

Edwards claimed that all of his sermons—and there were many on the subject of hell, some even more vivid than the one he preached in Enfield—were modeled on the admonition of the apostle Paul, "Knowing therefore the terror of the Lord, we persuade men" (2 Corinthians 5:11 KJV).

That kind of pastoral concern and evangelistic passion enabled Edwards to lend wise leadership and direction to the Great Awakening—perhaps the most sweeping revival in modern history. It enabled him to become the "acknowledged dean" of American Evangelicalism.[30] And it thrust him into the international limelight alongside Whitefield and Wesley as a spokesman for Christian unity and cooperation.

Even so, the controversy stirred by his determined commitment to an unadulterated proclamation of the Gospel never entirely went away. After nearly a quarter century of service to his Northampton congregation, a small disgruntled faction—advocates of what historian Perry Miller called a kind of "early pluralism" who desired less stringent moral standards for church membership than Edwards would allow—secured his ouster.[31] They

were apparently offended by his insistence that the message of justice—temporal and eternal—was inseparable from the message of
faith. He was exiled to the frontier where he lived out his days as a
missionary to the Indians.

But he had no regrets. He knew that the biblical imperative of
justice is not a matter to be trifled with. He knew that both the
imminence and the finality of eternal judgment mitigated against
lowering the standards, diluting the ethics, or compromising the
integrity of temporal judgment. He knew that hell was the best
argument against muddled and mitigated morals.

And yet, the controversy still rages. The argument continues
apace.

Truth, Justice, and the American Way

The Good News is that the bad news is bad—and yet hope
remains. Knowing this, Jonathan Edwards threw caution to the
wind and pled for his congregation to hear and heed the Gospel.

And so ought we to plead with all men.

But we don't. If we issue any warning at all, it is a self-conscious,
uncertain one—more often than not couched in the compromise
of pluralism. We almost act as if we were indifferent to the fate of
the myriads of men and nations.

J. I. Packer has lamented:

> At no time, perhaps, since the Reformation have Christians as a
> body been so unsure, tentative, and confused as to what they
> should believe and do. Certainty about the great issues of
> Christian faith and conduct is lacking all along the line. The out-
> side observer sees us as staggering on from gimmick to gimmick
> and stunt to stunt like so many drunks in a fog, not knowing at all
> where we are or which way we should be going. Preaching is hazy;
> heads are muddled; hearts fret; doubts drain our strength; uncer-
> tainty paralyzes action.[32]

As Ben Jackson said to me, most of us are not too sure that we
can be both successful and faithful in America today. And so like
the people in the days of Micah the prophet we cry, "Do not speak
out," and "Do not prophesy about these things" (Micah 2:6). We
shy away from the harsh truth—thinking that surely the Word of
the Lord only brings "good things" (Micah 2:7).

We want to present the world with an upbeat message. We
want to create a positive image. We want to emphasize the many
and substantial benefits of the Christian life. We want to put on a
happy face. We want to proclaim a Gospel of "peace."

The problem is "there is no peace for the wicked" (Isaiah 48:22).

A. W. Tozer decries this accommodated version of the Gospel
as a "spiteful cruelty to the lost and languishing—a cruelty mis-
guidedly offered in the name of comfort."[33] Furthermore:

> It gears him into a cleaner and jollier way of living and saves his
> self-respect. To the self-assertive it says, "Come and assert yourself
> for Christ." To the egotist it says, "Come and do your boasting in
> the Lord." To the thrill-seeker it says, "Come and enjoy the thrill
> of the Christian life." The idea behind this kind of thing may be
> sincere, but its sincerity does not save it from being false.[34]

Is there any wonder then that our influence is so slight in this
day of great need? Instead of nurturing God's people with the rich
truths of practical biblical instruction, we have indulged in theological junk food. Instead of building every discipline on the unwavering foundation of God's Word, we have humored ourselves with
intellectual white elephants. Instead of standing for justice in this
day of grave injustice, we have hidden the offense of the Gospel in
the evangelical ghetto.

If we refuse to expose the evil deeds of darkness in our day,
announce God's just wrath, and proclaim the only certain hope,
not only are the innocent and the helpless sure to perish, but God's
vast army will face one debilitating defeat after another.

It is unbelievable that the message of pluralism sounds to us
"more loving and Christ-like" than the once-common warnings of
perdition, judgment, and divine justice. It is a frightful thing that
we are more at home with the pleasant, non-confrontational, least-
common-denominator messages and methodologies of our culture
than we are with the holy alarms of Scripture. It is a senseless
tragedy that we have carelessly foisted the fierce injustice of our
own caution upon a hell-bound world.

Thus, G. K. Chesterton remarked: "If the world grows too
worldly, it can be rebuked by the church; but if the church grows
too worldly, it cannot be adequately rebuked for worldliness by
the world."[35]

The Micah Mandate provokes us to an unflinching demonstration of justice—in both word and deed—that not only guards our culture from the awful errors of pluralism, but that also guards all those within the culture from any grand illusions about the awful horrors of perdition as well.

THE FAITH THE JUST LIVE BY

"He has showed you, O man, what is good.
And what does the Lord require of you? To
act justly and to love mercy and to walk
humbly with your God" (Micah 6:8).

One of the marks of the faithful church through the ages has been an unflinching commitment to biblical standards of justice. Even when that commitment was slighted, scoffed, and scorned, the heroes of the faith stood their ground and asserted that ours was a moral universe created by a moral God and that His moral decrees were not to be trifled with but at great cost. Examples abound:

John Chrysostom (347–407) was one of the greatest preachers of the Patristic Age. His many extant sermons on family life, personal holiness, and Christian social responsibility remain models of wise teaching and faithful exposition while his liturgical reforms continue to define the parameters of orthodox worship to this day. A champion of charity to the poor, mercy to the lost, and tenderheartedness to the outcast, he was plainspoken about the ills and excesses of his day. As a result, though he was extremely popular among the people, his forthrightness earned him the enmity of many rich and powerful officials in the Byzantine court, including the Empress. Eventually he was exiled and put through innumerable humiliations. Throughout his ordeals, though, he remained steadfast, and even after his death, his impact upon the whole fabric of Byzantine culture was profoundly felt.

Bernard of Clairveaux (1090–1153) was one of the most brilliant Christian apologists, theologians, and reformers of the high medieval period as well as the inspirational composer of innumerable hymns including the beloved, *O Sacred Head Now Wounded*. A determined holy life, a commitment to charitable compassion, and an unusual eloquence earned Bernard a reputation in his day as a wise and astute counselor to kings, emperors, and popes. Even so, his willingness to embrace unpopular truths often made his high profile a precarious position. His ardor for biblical justice combined with his passion for peace made him a key player in most of the great events of his day: monastic establishments, agrarian reforms, peasant revolts, ecclesiastical reconciliations, Teutonic crusades, and attempts to liberate Jerusalem and the old Christian realms of the East.

William Jennings Bryan (1860–1925) was an American statesman who attempted to translate his strong Christian convictions into a coherent program of justice in both the private practice of law and the public political arena. He was catapulted to fame during the 1896 Democratic National Convention following a stirring populist speech entitled the *Cross of Gold*. His party adopted his progressive agenda to bring the promise of justice to every American and eventually nominated him as its presidential candidate three times—in 1896, 1900, and 1908. He stood against vested interests, powerful lobbies, and moneyed manipulators to advocate the cause of the ordinary citizen. Though he was narrowly defeated each time he ran, he remained one of the most popular and influential advocates of applying the principles of genuine biblical justice to every arena of life and culture. Though his name is most often remembered for his connection with the infamous *Scopes* evolution trial, he was known as a champion of justice in his own time.

Dozens of others could be cited throughout the wide span of history: Fabiola Fabii (d. 399), Dympna Caelrhynn (d. 682), Elizabeth of Portugal (d. 1336), Charles Borromeo (d. 1584), Henry Martyn (d. 1812), Elizabeth Fry (d. 1845), and Robert Caldwell (d. 1891). Each took a bold stand for that which was good, and just and true. Each risked the ire of all those around them who took offense at unvarnished biblical truth.

And as a result, each remains a paragon of courage and virtue even today.

DOING JUSTICE

"He has showed you, O man, what is good.
And what does the Lord require of you? To act
justly and to love mercy and to walk humbly
with your God" (Micah 6:8).

Survey the messages of the Minor Prophets—from Hosea to Malachi—and notice how often the issue of justice recurs. Then read the Sermon on the Mount or the Epistle of James to see how these themes are woven into the message of the New Testament.

It is easy to talk about justice in the abstract. To make the issue more practical and tangible, consider starting a list of all the kinds of questions the Bible addresses in terms of justice—from care of the poor to the protection of the innocent. Then assess how your life and faith stack up when it comes to "doing justice."

Do you know someone—perhaps someone in your church—who holds a strong commitment to justice? Maybe the person is involved in the pro-life movement, or volunteers at the local shelter for the homeless, or works on behalf of Christian political candidates. Have you ever asked the person how or why he or she got started? Perhaps the person would consider walking you through the process of deciding how best to get involved in doing justice yourself. Strike up a friendship. Discover what it is that makes the person tick—it may be one of the best decisions you've ever made.

Do you see a need that has not been addressed? Get busy. Go to work.

Notes

1. D. Martyn Lloyd-Jones, *The Heart of the Gospel* (Wheaton, Ill.: Crossway, 1991), 62.

2. *The Journal of Invective*, Spring 1992.

3. Oswald Chambers, *The Best from All His Works* (Nashville, Tenn.: Oliver Nelson, 1989), II:213.

4. John Callio, *Pluralism* (New York: Academia, 1990), 6.

5. Ibid.

6. Ibid.

7. James Dobson and Gary Bauer, *Children at Risk* (Dallas: Word, 1990).

8. James Davison Hunter, *Culture Wars* (New York: Basic Books, 1991).

9. C. S. Lewis, *Surprised by Joy* (New York: Macmillan, 1970), 14.

10. Jerry Kirk, *The Mind Polluters* (Nashville, Tenn.: Thomas Nelson, 1985), 34–35.

11. Reid Carpenter, *Pittsburgh Leadership Foundation* (Pittsburgh: PLF, 1988), 19.

12. *Report of the Attorney General* (Nashville, Tenn.: Rutledge Hill, 1986).

13. Walter Evans, *The Bordellos of Nevada* (Reno, Nev.: Desert Visitor, 1979).

14. *Coral Ridge Impact*, May 1990.

15. See William Bennett, *Index of Leading Cultural Indicators* (New York: Simon and Schuster, 1994).

16. *New York Newsday*, 2 February 1988.

17. E. Carrington Boggin, *The Rights of Gay People* (New York: Bantam, 1983).

18. *Fort Lauderdale Sun Sentinel*, 14 May 1989.

19. *Christian Observer*, Spring 1988.

20. Aleksandr Solzhenitsyn, *A Warning to the West* (New York: Harper and Row, 1978), 64.

21. James Q. Wilson, *The Moral Sense* (New York: Free Press, 1993), ix.

22. James Carlyle, *Jonathan Edwards* (Edinburgh, U.K.: Light and Life, 1962), 21.

23. Ibid., 23.

24. Ibid.

25. Arthur Eastman, Caesar Blake, et al., eds., *The Norton Reader: An Anthology of Expository Prose* (New York: Norton, 1965), 1108.

26. Garland Ferry, Basic Hermeneutics (Philadelphia: American Reformed Convention, 1929), 162.

27. John Gerstner, *The Rational Biblical Theology of Jonathan Edwards* (Powhatan, Va.: Berea, 1991), I:14.

28. Ibid., 4.

29. John Gerstner, *Repent or Perish* (Ligonier, Pa.: Soli Deo Gloria, 1990), 27–29.

30. Carlyle, *Edwards*, 21.

32. *Eklesia*, XV: 231.

33. A. W. Tozer, *The Old Cross and the New* (Gary, Ind.: Alliance, 1961), 4.

34. Ibid.

35. G. K. Chesterton, *Omnibus* (Sheed and Ward, 1938), 149.

MERCY: TO DO GOOD

The difference between approving laws,
and obeying them is frequently forgotten.
Samuel Johnson

LIVING AS IF PEOPLE MATTERED

*One of the strangest disparities of history lies
between the sense of abundance felt by older
and simpler societies and the sense of scarcity
felt by the ostensibly richer societies of today.*
Richard Weaver

I remember only too well the first time I met Francis Schaeffer. In 1979 I was puttering around in one of my favorite used bookstores—on Locust Street, just a couple of blocks from the beautiful and magnificent Christ Church Cathedral in downtown St. Louis. The cathedral is a vivid reminder of the remarkable flowering of creativity and beauty that the Gospel has always provoked through the ages.

Just out of sight of the great Easter pinnacle is a little row of quirky stores and businesses. There are a couple of musty antique dealers, a disreputable-looking chili restaurant, a jaunty coffee shop, a boutique specializing in platform shoes from the seventies, and, of course, the bookstore—stocking a rather eccentric jumble of old magazines, cheap paperbacks, and fine first editions arranged in no apparent order.

I had just discovered a good hardback copy of Scott's *Ivanhoe* and a wonderful turn-of-the-century pocket edition of Ruskin's *Seven Lamps of Architecture*—both for less than the cost of new paperback copies—when I rounded a corner and bumped into Dr. Schaeffer. Literally.

I had been reading his books since the late sixties and looked to him as my spiritual and intellectual mentor. Not only did he

express his orthodox Reformed faith in a clear and thoughtful fashion, his appreciation for the great heritage of Christendom's art,
music, and ideas and his commitment to practical justice and true
spirituality made him a beacon light of hope to me. In 1948, he
had gone to live in the Swiss Alps just below Villars. There, in a
little mountain chalet, he established a unique missionary outreach
to all who might find their way to his door.

Over the years, thousands of students, skeptics, and searchers
found their way to that door. He named the ministry L'Abri—a
French word meaning shelter—an apt description for the function
it served to the rootless generation of the Cold War era. It had
always seemed to me that L'Abri was precisely the kind of witness
that the church at the end of the twentieth century desperately
needed.

I'd like to say that as I stood face-to-face with my hero, I was
able to articulate my appreciation for all that he had done for my
faith and my walk with Christ. I'd like to say that I was able to
express my gratitude and then perhaps strike up a stimulating conversation about, say, epistemological self-consciousness. I'd like to
say that as providence afforded me the opportunity I was able to
think of all the questions I'd always wanted answered.

Unfortunately, that was not the case.

Instead, the first thought that sprang into my mind was: "Oh
my, he's short!"

My second thought was: "What a haircut!"

My third thought was: "And what's the deal with the knickers?"

In shock, I realized that I couldn't think of a single intelligent
thing to say. I had fallen epistemologically unconscious.

Evidently, Dr. Schaeffer could read the awkward consternation
in my eyes. He chuckled, introduced himself to me, and struck up
a conversation. Amidst my embarrassed bumfuddlement he was
cheerfully gracious and kind. He commended me on my selections
and then showed me a couple other books he thought I might
like—a fine paperback copy of Van Til's *The Calvinistic Concept of
Culture* and a rare edition of Schaff's *The Principle of Protestantism*.

Here was one of the brightest minds of our generation giving
his time and attention to a gawky young Christian who couldn't
even string together a coherent sentence. I later discovered that
this was typical of him. Though he was often passionate, stubborn,

and irascible, his life was suffused with a clear sense of calling—a calling to serve others. He demonstrated that calling on a daily basis—not just through heroic feats of sacrifice but through the quiet virtue of ordinary kindness. He believed that the Reformation doctrine of the priesthood of all believers was best portrayed in the beauty of caring human relationships. And so he listened. He cared. He gave. He put into motion Christ's tender mercies through the simplest acts of humble service.

I came away from that first brief encounter with Dr. Schaeffer with an entirely new understanding of biblical mercy. With a servant's heart, he treated me as if I mattered. He treated me the way we are all to treat one another.

Service

Service is a much ballyhooed concept these days. The literature of business success and personal management tosses it about rather profligately.

We are told, for instance, that our industrial economy has been almost completely transformed into a service economy by the advent of the information age. The service factor is the new by-word for success in the crowded global marketplace. Good service guarantees customer loyalty, management efficiency, and employee morale. It provides a competitive edge for companies in an increasingly cut-throat business environment. It is the means toward empowerment, flexibility, and innovation at a time when those qualities are essential for business survival. It prepares ordinary men and women to out-sell, out-manage, out-motivate, and out-negotiate their competition. It enables them to "swim with the sharks without being eaten alive."[1]

According to Jack Eckerd and Chuck Colson, service on the job and in the workplace can mean many things: "Valuing workers. Managing from the trenches. Communicating. Inspiring excellence. Training. Using profits to motivate."[2]

Virtually all the corporate prognosticators, strategic forecasters, motivational pundits, and management consultants agree—from Tom Peters, John Naisbitt, and Stephen Covey to Richard Foster, Michael Gerber, and Zig Ziglar. They all say that service is an indispensable key to success in business or success in life.

According to these analysts, service in business is essentially a complex combination of common courtesy, customer satisfaction, and the "spirit of enterprise." It is simply realizing that the customer is always right and then going the extra mile. It is a principle-centered approach to human relationships and community respon-sibilities. It is putting first things first.[3]

Biblical service is a priestly function of mercy.

This new emphasis on service is not just confined to the corpo-rate world. It has also suddenly reappeared as a stock-in-trade public virtue in the discourse of politics. Candidates now offer themselves for public service rather than to merely run for office. They invoke cheery images of community service, military ser-vice, and civic service as evidence of their suitability to govern the affairs of state. Once in office they initiate vast federal pro-grams for national service. They charge the lumbering govern-ment bureaucracy with the task of domestic service. And they offer special recognition for citizens who have performed exem-plary volunteer service.

Again, service is defined rather broadly in a series of happy platitudes—as an expansive sense of public-spiritedness, good neighborliness, community-mindedness, or big-hearted coopera-tiveness.

All of these things are certainly admirable. They are fine and good as far as they go. But they are not at all what the Bible has in mind when it speaks of service—as Francis Schaeffer would no doubt have readily attested.

Biblical service isn't a tactic designed to boost profit margins, protect market shares, keep customers happy, or improve employee relations. It isn't a strategy designed to inculcate patrio-tism, strengthen community relations, or attract more investments. It is not a technique to pad resumes, garner votes, or patronize constituents. It isn't a style of leadership, a personality bent, or a habit of highly effective people.

Instead, biblical service is a priestly function of mercy. The Hebrew word often used for service in the Old Testament is *sharath*. It literally means "to minister" or "to treat with affection."

Similarly, in the New Testament the Greek word *diakoneo* is often used. It literally means "to care for" or to "offer relief." In both cases, the priestly connotations and the merciful intentions of service are quite evident. In both cases, the emphasis is on the interpersonal dimension rather than the institutional dimension, on mercy rather than management, on true righteousness rather than mere rightness. Biblical service is far more concerned about taking care of souls than about taking care of business.

God cares for the needy.
And His people are to do likewise.

This distinction between the ministry of service and the business of service is like the difference between faith in God and faith in faith.[4]

Doing Unto Others

God is merciful and just.

He works righteousness and justice for all. Morning by morning, He dispenses His justice without fail and without partiality. All his ways are just, so that injustice is an abomination to Him.

Thus, He is adamant about ensuring the cause of the abused, the meek, and the weak. Time after time, Scripture stresses this important attribute of God:

> The Lord abides forever; He has established His throne for judgment, and He will judge the world in righteousness; He will execute judgment for the peoples with equity. The Lord also will be a stronghold for the oppressed, a stronghold in times of trouble. (Psalm 9:7–9 NASB)

> "Because of the oppression of the weak and the groaning of the needy, I will now arise," says the Lord. "I will protect them from those who malign them." (Psalm 12:5)

> A father to the fatherless, a defender of widows, is God in his holy dwelling. God sets the lonely in families, he leads forth the prisoners with singing; but the rebellious live in a sun-scorched land. (Psalm 68:5–6)

God cares for the needy. And His people are to do likewise.

If God has comforted us, then we are to comfort others. If God has forgiven us, then we are to forgive others. If God has loved us, then we are to love others. If He has taught us, then we are to teach others. If He has borne witness to us, then we are to bear witness to others. If He has laid down His life for us, then we are to lay down our lives for one another.[5]

Whenever God commanded the priestly nation of Israel to imitate Him in ensuring justice for the wandering homeless, the alien, and the sojourner, He reminded them that they were once despised, rejected, and homeless themselves. It was only by the grace and mercy of God that they had been redeemed from that low estate. Thus they were to exercise compassion to the broken-hearted and the dispossessed. They were to serve.

Priestly privilege brings priestly responsibility. If Israel refused to take up that responsibility, then God would revoke their privilege. If they refused to exercise reciprocal mercy, then God would rise up in His anger to visit the land with His wrath and displeasure, expelling them into the howling wilderness once again. On the other hand, if they fulfilled their calling to live lives of merciful service, then they would ever be blessed.[6]

The principle still holds true. Those of us who have received the compassion of the Lord on High are to demonstrate tenderness in kind to all those around us. This is precisely the lesson Jesus was driving at in the parable of the unmerciful slave (Matthew 18:23–35).

The moral of the parable is clear. The needy around us are living symbols of our own former helplessness and privation. We are therefore to be living symbols of God's justice, mercy, and compassion. We are to do as He has done. God has set the pattern by His gracious working in our lives. We are to follow that pattern by serving others in the power of the indwelling Spirit.

In other words, the Gospel calls us to live daily as if people really matter. It calls us to live lives of selfless concern. We are to pay attention to the needs of others. In both word and deed, in both thought and action we are to weave ordinary kindness into the very fabric of our lives.

But this kind of ingrained mercy goes far beyond mere politeness. We are to demonstrate concern for the poor. We are to show pity toward the weak. We are to rescue the afflicted from violence. We are to familiarize ourselves with the case of the helpless, give of our wealth, and share of our sustenance. We are to put on "compassion, kindness, humility, gentleness and patience" (Colossians 3:12). We are to take up "the case of the stranger" (Job 29:16). We are to love our neighbors as ourselves (Mark 12:31) and "rescue those being led away to death" (Proverbs 24:11–12).

According to the Scriptures, this kind of comprehensive servanthood emphasis is, in fact, a primary indication of the authenticity of our faith: "Religion that God our Father accepts as pure and faultless is this: to look after orphans and widows in their distress and to keep oneself from being polluted by the world" (James 1:27).

We are called to do "righteousness and justice" (Genesis 18:19 NASB). We are to be ministers of God's peace, instruments of His love, and ambassadors of His kingdom. We are to care for the helpless, feed the hungry, clothe the naked, shelter the homeless, visit the prisoner, and protect the innocent. We are to live lives of merciful service.

Good Deeds

In writing to Titus, the young pastor of Crete's pioneer church, the apostle Paul pressed home this fundamental truth with a clear sense of persistence and urgency. The task before Titus was not an easy one. Cretan culture was terribly worldly. It was marked by deceit, ungodliness, sloth, and gluttony (Titus 1:12). Thus, Paul's instructions were precise. Titus was to preach the glories of grace, but he was also to make good deeds evident. Priestly mercy and selfless servanthood were to be central priorities in his new work:

> For the grace of God has appeared, bringing salvation to all men, instructing us to deny ungodliness and worldly desires and to live sensibly, righteously and godly in the present age, looking for the blessed hope and the appearing of the glory of our great God and Savior, Christ Jesus; who gave Himself for us, that He might redeem us from every lawless deed and purify for Himself a people for His own possession, zealous for good deeds. (Titus 2:11–14 NASB)

Paul tells Titus he should build his entire fledgling ministry around works of mercy: He was to be an example of good deeds (Titus 2:7). He was to teach the people to watch for chances to do good (3:1). They were all to "learn to devote themselves to doing what is good, in order that they might provide for daily necessities and not live unproductive lives" (3:14). Some within the church professed to know God, "but by their actions they deny him. They are detestable, disobedient and unfit for doing anything good" (1:16). Titus was to "rebuke them sharply, so that they will be sound in the faith" (1:13).

As a pastor, Titus had innumerable tasks that he was responsible to fulfill. He had administrative duties, doctrinal duties, discipling duties, preaching duties, counseling duties, and arbitrating duties. But intertwined with them all, fundamental to them all, were his servanthood duties.

To the Uttermost

Paul called himself a servant (Galatians 1:10). Similarly, James, Peter, Epaphroditus, Timothy, Abraham, Moses, David, and Daniel were all called servants.[7] In fact, even before they were called "Christians," all of the first century believers were called "servants" (1 Corinthians 7:22).

Whenever and wherever the Gospel has gone out, the faithful have emphasized the priority of good works, especially works of compassion toward the needy. Every great revival in the history of the church, from Paul's missionary journeys to the Reformation, from the Alexandrian outreach of Athanasius to the Great Awakening in America, has been accompanied by an explosion of priestly service. Hospitals were established. Orphanages were founded. Rescue missions were started. Almshouses were built. Soup kitchens were begun. Charitable societies were incorporated. The hungry were fed, the naked clothed, and the unwanted rescued. Word was wed to deeds.[8]

This fact has always proven to be the bane of the church's enemies. Unbelievers can argue theology. They can dispute philosophy. They can subvert history. And they can undermine character. But they are helpless in the face of extraordinary feats of selfless compassion.[9]

Thus, Martin Luther said: "Where there are no good works,

there is no faith. If works and love do not blossom forth, it is not genuine faith, the Gospel has not yet gained a foothold, and Christ is not yet rightly known."[10]

Likewise, the *Westminster Confession* asserted:

> Good works, done in obedience to God's commandments, are the fruits and evidences of a true and lively faith: and by them believers manifest their thankfulness, strengthen their assurance, edify their brethren, adorn the profession of the Gospel, stop the mouths of the adversaries, and glorify God whose workmanship they are.[11]

All too often in our own day though, we have tended to decline those priestly responsibilities—yielding the work of service to government bureaucrats or professional philanthropists. Grave societal dilemmas that have always busied the church before—like defending the sanctity of life, caring for the aged, and protecting the helpless—have been mentally and practically separated from our other "spiritual" responsibilities. They have been relegated to the status of "issues," even declared "political" and put on the other side of the fence from us in "the separation of church and state."

From a biblical perspective, though, these things are not "issues"; they cannot be separated from our tasks as believer-priests. They are our tasks as believer-priests. They *are* central to our purpose and calling in the world.

Many Christians have observed—only partly in jest—that if God doesn't judge America soon, He's probably going to have to apologize to Sodom and Gomorrah. That may well be true—but not for the reason that we think. God did not judge Sodom and Gomorrah because of their rampant greed, perversity, and corruption. He judged them because, as discussed in chapter 9, those who were charged with serving didn't (Ezekiel 16:49–50). If God's wrath ever does utterly consume America, it will be for precisely the same reason. When biblical service is replaced by its worldly counterfeits, the effects go far beyond rising taxes, bloated bureaucracies, welfare graft, urban blight, and sundered families. When we fail to do the priestly work of mercy and compassion, judgment becomes inevitable.

Sava of Trnova, writing at the end of the seventh century, said:

> The chief spiritual works in the world are sevenfold: to admonish

sinners, to instruct the ignorant, to counsel the doubtful, to comfort the sorrowful, to suffer wrongs patiently, to forgive injuries,
and to pray for all men at all times. Thus, we are to feed the hungry, give drink to the thirsty, to clothe the naked, to ransom the
captives, to shelter the homeless, to visit the sick, and to rescue
the perishing, for only in these corporal acts of service may this
world of carnality be guarded from the full consequences of judgment.[12]

The Bible tells us that if we will obey the command to be gener-
ous to the poor, we ourselves will taste joy. If we will serve the
needy, God will preserve us. If we will offer priestly mercy to the
afflicted, we ourselves will be spared. We will prosper, our desires
will be satisfied, and we will even be raised up from beds of sorrow
and suffering.[13] God will ordain peace for us, authenticate our
faith, and bless our witness to the world.[14]

But only if we will serve.

Wherever committed Christians have gone . . . selfless care for the needy has been in evidence.

Charles Haddon Spurgeon, the great Victorian pastor, not only
was a masterful pulpiteer, administrator, writer, and evangelist, he
was a determined champion of the deprived and the rejected. He
gave more than half of his incredibly busy schedule to one or
another of the sixty organizations or institutions he founded for
their care and comfort. Explaining his furious activity on behalf of
the poor and needy, Spurgeon said:

> God's intent in endowing any person with more substance than he
> needs is that he may have the pleasurable office, or rather the
> delightful privilege, of relieving want and woe. Alas, how many
> there are who consider that store which God has put into their
> hands on purpose for the poor and needy, to be only so much pro-
> vision for their excessive luxury, a luxury which pampers them but
> yields them neither benefit nor pleasure.[15]

Wherever committed Christians have gone, throughout Europe,
into the darkest depths of Africa, to the outer reaches of China,

along the edges of the American frontier, and beyond to the
Australian outback, selfless care for the needy has been in evidence. In fact, most of the church's greatest heroes are those who
willingly gave the best of their lives to the less fortunate. Service
was their hallmark. Mercy was their emblem.

A Life of Service

According to the majority of eighteenth- and nineteenth-
century historians, the most remarkable event during America's
founding era did not take place on a battlefield. It did not occur
during the course of the constitutional debates. It was not recorded during the great diplomatic negotiations with France, Spain, or
Holland. It did not take place at sea, or in the assemblies of the
states, or in the counsels of war.

In a humble demonstration of servanthood, the field command-
er of the continental armies surrendered his commission to the
congressional authorities at Annapolis.

At the time, he was the idol of the country and his soldiers. The
army was unpaid, and the veteran troops, well-armed and fresh
from their victory at Yorktown, were eager to have him take control of the disordered country. Some wanted to crown him king.
Others thought to make him a dictator—rather like Cromwell had
been a century earlier in England.

With the loyal support of the army and the enthusiasm of the
populace, it would have been easy enough for him to have made
himself the ruler of the new nation. But instead, General George
Washington resigned his officer's commission. He appeared before
President Thomas Mifflin and his cabinet and submitted himself to
their governance.

Though he had often wrangled in disagreement with his superi-
ors over matters of military strategy, pay schedules, supply ship-
ments, troop deployment, and the overlap of civil and martial
responsibilities, there was never any question of his ultimate loyalty or allegiance. In the end, he always submitted himself to the
authority God had placed over him.

And that was no mean feat.

Washington had faithfully served under eleven different
American presidents at a time of severest crisis. The first two held

office prior to the signing of the Declaration of Independence—
Peyton Randolph of Virginia and Henry Middleton of South
Carolina. The next six held office between the time of the
Declaration and the ratification of the first constitution—John
Hancock of Massachusetts, Henry Laurens of South Carolina,
John Jay of New York, Samuel Huntington of Connecticut, Samuel
Johnson of North Carolina, and Thomas McKean of Delaware.
The last three held office under the Articles of Confederation—
John Hanson of Maryland, Elias Budinot of New Jersey, and final-
ly, Thomas Mifflin of Pennsylvania. Another four presidents would
hold office during Washington's short interlude away from public
life prior to the ratification of the current constitution—Richard
Henry Lee of Virginia, Nathaniel Gorham of Massachusetts,
Arthur St. Clair of Pennsylvania, and Cyrus Griffin of Virginia.
During all those trying days, under each of those varied men,
General Washington gave himself wholeheartedly to the loyal task
of selfless service.

He obeyed orders. He rendered due respect. He yielded to the
authority of lawful office and jurisdiction. He met the needs of the
hour. He set aside personal ambition, preference, security, and at
times, personal opinion in order to serve.

Where there is mercy
there is hope.

"His true greatness was evidenced," said the pundit Henry
Adams, "in the fact that he never sought greatness, but rather service."[16] The dean of American historians, Francis Parkman, con-
curred that it was this "remarkable spirit of the servant" that ultimately "elevated him even higher in his countrymen's estimations
than he already was."[17]

George Washington lived a life of service. He practiced what
we today call servant-leadership. He would settle for nothing less.
He would strive for nothing more. And he left the disposition of
the matter of his life and fortune in the hands of God.

Though we generally think of mercy more in terms of charity or
philanthropy, Washington's balanced and selfless perspective actu-

ally comes closer to the biblical ideal. Kindness, helpfulness, compassion, and care are the natural outgrowths of a servant's heart. Where personal ambition and a lust for self-fulfillment are subdued, true mercy is sure to follow.

Good Service

The prophet Micah condemned the people of his day for their heartless defrauding and victimizing of the needy (Micah 2:1–2). He asserted that the imminent judgment of their land was due to their tolerance of sin, their blatant selfishness, and their refusal to undertake their servanthood responsibilities (3:2–4). Instead, they were concerned only with their own comforts and pleasures (2:8–11). They were intent on their own personal peace and affluence, often at the cost of oppression and exploitation (3:5–11). They had thus violated the covenant (5:10–15).

Where there is no mercy there is no hope.

Thus, the Micah Mandate was not only a call to the people to repent and to return to the path of righteousness, it was a proclamation of reconciliation and healing. It was a promise of better things to come. The prophet asserted that the remnant would be regathered (Micah 4:6). The shame of affliction would be lifted (4:7). And the lost fortunes of the land would be restored (4:8).

Where there is mercy there is hope.

Therefore let us too be "zealous for good deeds" (Titus 2:14 NASB).

ZEALOUS FOR GOOD DEEDS

"He has showed you, O man, what is good. And what does the Lord require of you? To act justly and to love mercy and to walk humbly with your God"
(Micah 6:8).

Through the ages, the great heroes of the faith were notable as much for their charity and kindness as they were for their doctrinal fidelity. They were invariably men and women of mercy who lived lives of selfless service. Examples abound:

Not only did *John Wyclif* (1329–84) revive interest in the

Scriptures during a particularly dismal and degenerate era with his translation of the New Testament into English, he also unleashed a grassroots movement of lay preachers and relief workers that brought hope to the poor for the first time since the peasants' land had been taken more than two generations before. Those common Lollards—as they were most often called—carried Wyclif's determined message of grace and mercy to the entire kingdom, laying the foundations for the Reformation in England more than a century and a half later.

John Calvin (1509–64) established Geneva as the epicenter of the Reformation with his profound theological insight and his rich devotional piety. His careful and systematic codification of the biblical foundations for Reform was like a magnet for the best and brightest throughout Christendom. The city quickly became an island of intellectual integrity and economic prosperity. In addition, though, it became renowned for its charitable compassion. It was a kind of safe haven for all of Europe's poor and persecuted, dispossessed and distressed. There they found that Calvin had not only instructed the people in such things as the providence of God, but he had also taught them the importance of mercy in balancing the Christian life.

Dwight L. Moody (1837–99) was America's foremost evangelist throughout the difficult days that immediately followed the cataclysm of the War Between the States and disruption of Reconstruction. Literally thousands came to know Christ because the former shoe salesman faithfully proclaimed the Gospel wherever and whenever he had opportunity—pioneering the methods of both modern crusade evangelism and Sunday-school outreach. But in addition to preaching to the masses, he cared for the masses. He was responsible for the establishment of some one hundred and fifty schools, street missions, soup kitchens, clinics, colportage societies, and other charitable organizations. He believed it was essential that Christians proclaim the Gospel in both word and deed. As a result, his impact on the nation is still felt—through many of those institutions that continue their vital work—nearly a century after his death.

Dozens of others could be cited throughout the wide span of history: Polycarp (d. 155), Ambrose (d. 397), Angelica of Brescia (d. 1540), Edmund Arrowsmith (d. 1628) David Brainerd (d. 1747), George Mueller (d. 1898), and Florence Nightingale (d. 1910). Each made the priestly message of their lips manifest by the servanthood message of their hands. Thus, each became an emblem of mercy in this often merciless world.

DO A GOOD TURN DAILY

"He has showed you, O man, what is good.
And what does the Lord require of you? To act
justly and to love mercy and to walk humbly
with your God" (Micah 6:8).

An entire catalog of Scriptural exhorts us to act
mercifully to those around us.[18] Do a brief concord-
ance study—looking up the verses that deal with
mercy, kindness, and compassion—to get a good
overview of the subject. Try to make a list—from
memory, if possible—of all the saints and heroes of
the past whose stories of mercy, service, and compassion you have heard in sermons, Sunday school,
missions conferences, Bible studies, or devotions.
What does your list tell you about the import and
impact of mercy ministry on the overall history of
the church? There are needs all around us. It
doesn't matter what section of the country we live
in. It doesn't matter what kind of neighborhood we
call home. Single mothers silently struggle to make
ends meet. Elderly couples try to get by on fixed
incomes. Young families are stymied by debt,
underemployment, illiteracy, physical handicaps, or
prejudice. There are undernourished and poorly
clothed children, third- and fourth-generation welfare dependents. There are hurting, lonely, desperate people. They may be right next door, down the
street, around the block, across the tracks, or on
the other side of town. But they are there. Stop.
Look. Listen. See if you can't develop new eyes to
see those needs where they are. Now, get busy.
You may not have abundant resources or even
much time to spare, but none of us is too strapped
to care about—and then do something about—the
needs of others.

Notes

1. *Houston Chronicle*, 18 May 1986; *Forbes*, 14 September 1992; *Forbes*, 9 September 1993; *Wall Street Journal*, 16 April 1992; Harvey Mackay, *Swim with the Sharks* (New York: William Morrow, 1988), 1.

2. Chuck Colson and Jack Eckerd, *Why America Doesn't Work* (Dallas: Word, 1991), 168.

3. George Gilder, *The Spirit of Enterprise* (New York: Simon and Schuster, 1984); Michael Gerber, *Power Point* (New York: HarperCollins, 1991); Tom Peters, *Thriving on Chaos* (New York: Knopf, 1987); Stephen Covey, Roger Merrill, and Rebecca Merrill, *First Things First* (New York: Simon and Schuster, 1994).

4. Faith in God is personal and objective. Faith in faith is impersonal and subjective. Faith in God transcends self-interest and self-fulfillment. Faith in faith descends into self-reliance and self-assurance. Faith in God is a belief in Someone who has revealed Himself to man "at many times and in various ways" (Hebrews 1:1). Faith in faith is simply "a belief" in something or any thing (James 2:19).

5. To see these principles demonstrated in Scripture: 2 Corinthians 1:4; Ephesians 4:32; 1 John 4:11; Matthew 28:20; John 15:26–27; 1 John 3:16.

6. See Isaiah 1:11–17; Exodus 22:24; Psalm 41:1–2.

7. James 1:1; 2 Peter 1:1; Colossians 4:12; 2 Timothy 2:24; Psalm 105:42; Nehemiah 9:14; Psalm 89:3; Romans 6:20.

8. George Grant, *Bringing in the Sheaves: Transforming Poverty into Productivity* (Brentwood, Tenn.: Wolgemuth and Hyatt, 1985).

9. George Grant, *Third Time Around* (Brentwood, Tenn.: Wolgemuth and Hyatt, 1990).

10. John Dillenberger, ed., *Martin Luther* (New York: Doubleday, 1961), 18.

11. Confession, XVIII:2.

12. Terra Ecalivat, VI: 82.

13. Proverbs 14:21; Psalm 41:1–2; Proverbs 28:27; Proverbs 11:24; Proverbs 11:25; Psalm 41:3.

14. Isaiah 26:12; James 2:14–26; Isaiah 58:6–12.

15. George H. Neville, *Good Works* (Edinburgh, UK: McGavock, 1956), 202.

16. B. L. Cartwright, *Washington* (Boston: Little, Brown, 1924), 166.

17. Ibid.

18. The following list is by no means comprehensive, but it may provide you with a good starting place for personal study:

Exodus 22:25
Leviticus 19:10
Leviticus 23:22
Leviticus 25:35–37
Numbers 18:24
Deuteronomy 14:29
Deuteronomy 15:1–2
Deuteronomy 24:19–21
Ruth 2:1–23
Ruth 4:1–12
Psalm 41:1–3
Proverbs 11:25
Proverbs 14:21
Proverbs 14:31
Proverbs 17:5
Proverbs 21:13
Proverbs 22:9
Proverbs 28:27
Proverbs 29:7
Proverbs 31:8–9
Isaiah 1:10–17
Isaiah 10:1–2
Isaiah 32:6–8
Isaiah 58:1–12
Amos 5:1–27
Matthew 5:16
Matthew 7:12
Matthew 10:8

Matthew 25:31–46
Mark 12:44
Luke 3:11
Luke 6:38
Luke 9:48
Luke 10:30–37
Luke 11:41
Luke 12:33–34
Acts 20:35
Romans 12:8–20
2 Corinthians 1:3–4
2 Corinthians 8:1–24
2 Corinthians 9:7
Galatians 5:6
Galatians 6:2
Galatians 6:9–10
Ephesians 2:8–10
Ephesians 5:2
2 Thessalonians 3:6–10
1 Timothy 5:8
1 Timothy 6:18–19
Titus 2:11–14
Titus 3:1
Titus 3:8
Titus 3:14
Hebrews 13:16
James 2:14–26
1 John 3:17

ODDITIES AND RARITIES: ETHICS

We cannot expect a more cordial
welcome than disturbers of complacency
have received in any other age.
Richard Weaver

T he hot kelvin lights bore down on us. Cameras whirred. Production personnel bustled. The host prodded and cajoled. Nervous tension filled the air.

A staffer from the multi-billion-dollar abortion behemoth, Planned Parenthood, looked across the impeccable set and challenged me. "What I don't understand about you anti-choicers is where you've been all these years." The camera moved in to capture the high drama. Passion shone from her features. Beads of sweat trickled down her perfectly-sculpted brow. "Women have been suffering for centuries. The anti-abortion movement didn't even exist until 1973. You're just a bunch of extremists, opportunists, and Johnny-come-latelies."

I told her that the pro-life movement had actually existed since the days of early Christendom. The church has always stood against abortion, cannibalism, euthanasia, and ethnic cleansing. She insisted that I was indulging in wishful thinking, that the pro-life movement has lost and ought to recognize it is time to give up. I stood my ground and told her that public opinion is not our measure, that we will continue doing the work Christ has given us to do until He returns.

Cut. Break for commercial and the prerecorded outro wrap.

And my little pro-life contingent in the audience became unusually ecstatic.

I wasn't surprised that my sparring partner was a bit incensed. What caught me off guard was the reaction of my friends in the pro-life movement:

"Wow. I'd never heard *anything* like that before."

"Was there *really* a pro-life movement *before* 1973?"

"I didn't even know that abortion was an *issue* before Roe v. Wade."

"Do you really think that we will be able to stand firm until the end?"

We have practically lost sight of the fact that the church is a perpetually defeated thing that always survives its conquerors.

Over the next several months, as I traveled around the country working with pro-life leaders from virtually every major organization, across all ecclesiastical boundaries, and in every strata of life, I was rather astonished to discover a similar unfamiliarity with our rich heritage of mercy ministry—and a corresponding uncertainty about the future. People who had been valiant in defense of the innocent were generally unaware of the fact that the battle had already been fought and won—several times—by Christian pro-life stalwarts generations and even centuries ago.

I was entirely unprepared for that.

After all, here we were, decades into a ferocious new life-and-death struggle over abortion, infanticide, and euthanasia. How could we be so uninformed of our own legacy? How could we be unaware of the wealth of wisdom and experience from the past?

That so many of us have forgotten our heritage is bad enough, but what is worse is that because we have forgotten it, we have begun to lose the ability to see beyond our present difficulties and circumstances. And consequently, we have begun to lose heart.

Distracted by the oblivion of the moment, we have almost abandoned the crucial work at hand. We have begun to waver in the face of temporary setbacks and defeats. We have practically lost sight of the fact that the church is a perpetually defeated thing that always survives its conquerors. We have even started to despair of being able to hold on until the trumpet sounds.

And that is a dangerous situation. It makes our merciful work in the world all but impossible.

Winners and Losers

Everyone loves a winner. The sweet smell of success draws nearly all of us like moths to a candle flame. Popularity, celebrity, prominence, and fame are not only the hallmarks of our age, they are just about the only credentials we require for adulation or leadership.

As a result, we are generally not fond of the peculiar, the obscure, or the unpopular. At best we reserve pity for losers. We view with suspicion anyone who somehow fails to garner kudos from the world at large. If people have fallen prey to vilification, defamation, or humiliation we simply assume that they must somehow be at fault.

There was a time when martyrdom was among the church's highest callings and greatest honors. Early on, Christians embraced the truth that "everyone who wants to live a godly life in Christ Jesus will be persecuted" (2 Timothy 3:12). The heroes of the faith have always been those who sacrificed their lives, fortunes, and reputations for the sake of the Gospel.

But no longer. We attach almost a kind of shame to those who suffer persecution or isolation in our culture. If their cause does not meet with quick success, we abandon them. Maybe they didn't try hard enough. Maybe they just made a couple of dumb mistakes. Maybe they had faulty theology. Maybe they failed to marshal effective public-relations techniques. But however they got into the mess they're in, we are all but certain that they are not the kind of models we ought to follow.

E. M. Bounds, the great nineteenth-century pastor and evangelist who penned several classic books on prayer, asserted that too often "when the church prospers it loses sight of the very virtues from whence its prosperity has sprung." According to Bounds, those virtues "invariably have sprung out of either the suffering of believers or their response to the suffering of others."

That insight was honed from his own personal experience.

Throughout his long earthly service to Christ, Bounds suffered
both fierce persecution and enforced obscurity. During the calamitous War Between the States, he was imprisoned by Northern
troops—despite the fact that he was a loyal Unionist in a border
state—simply because he refused to surrender his congregation's
property to federal regulators. Later he suffered scorn at the hands
of liberal denominational administrators who objected to his
unswerving evangelical orthodoxy. Even at the end of his life, he
was unable to enjoy success—he was sorely neglected by publishing executives who believed that his brilliant doctrinal and devotional writings were too rigid, too legalistic, or too harsh. He was
beaten, ridiculed, defrocked, and defamed. He suffered poverty,
isolation, betrayal, and disgrace.

Through it all though, Bounds said that he found solace in the
fact that the Christian vocation does not depend on the confirma-
tion of worldly notions of success and thus does not need to adjust
to the ever-shifting tides of situation or circumstance. He knew
that the blood, toil, tears, and sweat of the faithful are the seeds of
real success.

Though that may be an alien notion to us today, it has been the
common experience of virtually all who have gone before us in
faith: apostles, prophets, martyrs, confessors, pastors, evangelists,
missionaries, reformers, and witnesses. They tasted the bittersweet
truth that the kingdom of heaven belongs to "those who are persecuted because of righteousness" (Matthew 5:10), and that great
blessings and rewards eventually await those who have been insult-
ed and slandered, who nevertheless persevere in their high callings
(Matthew 5:12).

And so, though they often suffered the ridicule and torments of
the world, they remained steadfast, continued their course, and
walked in grace. They did their jobs.

According to the Scriptures, it is incumbent upon us to "comfort
those in any trouble with the comfort which we ourselves have
received from God" (2 Corinthians 1:4). We are to "carry each
other's burdens, and in this way you will fulfill the law of Christ"
(Galatians 6:2). We are to "encourage one another and build each
other up" (1 Thessalonians 5:11). The mandate to care for one
another and all those who suffer—even in the midst of our own
travail—rings as clear as a clarion down through the ages.

The tenderest stories, the greatest adventures, and the most inspiring examples of faith across the wide span of history are invariably those instances when the Family of God has acted like a family and when the Household of Faith has functioned as a household. They have been when the church served as Christ's own instrument of mercy, when it became a kind of medicine of immortality to the dying minions of the world.

Strength to Stand

Like so many before him—and so many who would follow—E. M. Bounds discovered the beauty of fellowship, the strength of communion, and the brilliance of grace at a time when ugliness, weakness, and dullness seemed most certain to prevail in his life. "It was in those darkest hours" he would later write, "that the radiant glory of Christ's redemptive work was made plain to me through the commonest of courtesies conveyed by the brethren. It was then that the powerful solace of works of mercy became evident to me." Indeed, it was only as he witnessed the constant and fervent service of the church during his bitterest days of adversity that he began to comprehend the place and power of prayer—a comprehension that would in later years bring blessing and strength to generations of Christian readers through his incisive books.

Merciful service in the face of suffering is "often the glue that holds together the varied fragments of the confessing church" says the remarkable Romanian pastor Josef Tson. It affords the church "strong bonds of unity, compassion, and tenderheartedness" says Russian evangelist Georgi Vins. It "provokes the very best in us, demonstrating grace to a watching world, working out that which God has worked in," according to Indian apologist Vishal Mangalwadi. It "lays sure foundations for evangelism and discipleship simply because in the face of tyranny, oppression, and humiliation, the church has no option but to be the church," asserts Croatian pastor Josep Kulacik. "Disguised as evil, persecution comes to us as an ultimate manifestation of God's good providence" says Bosnian pro-life leader Frizof Gemielic. "It provokes us toward a new-found dependence upon His grace, upon His Word, and upon His people. It is in that sense a paradoxical blessing perhaps even more profound than prosperity."

Our response to the "fragrance of oppression," as historian Herbert Schlossberg has dubbed the persecutions and sufferings of our world, is perhaps the single most significant indicator of the health and vitality of the church. It is "in great endurance; in troubles, hardships and distresses; in beatings, imprisonments and riots; in hard work, sleepless nights and hunger" (2 Corinthians 6:4–5) that our mettle is proven.

Everyone loves a winner. That's not all bad—as long as our understanding of who the real winners are conforms to biblical standards.

But then that's the rub, isn't it?

Peer Pressure

It appears that Pogo was right: "We have met the enemy and he is us."[1]

> # We want the same salvation as in the Old Time Religion—but with half the hassle and a third less guilt.

We have so completely capitulated to worldly standards of success that the modern church is awash in compromise. Our flippant commitment to the contemporaniety, modernity, and fashionability of the world has made us nearly indistinguishable from any other social institution or philanthropic enterprise in America. Our mimicry of the world and the ways of the world has transformed virtually every aspect of ministry from pastoral care and foreign missions to church growth and Sunday worship. It is almost as if we've caught the spirit of the age like a virus. As a result, we are afflicted by what Kenneth Meyers calls a "plague of terminal trendiness."[2] It is no longer a joke: We have actually become the "church of what's happenin' now."[3]

The result is that even in evangelical congregations, the Gospel has been squeezed into the mold of this world with amazing ease. We tone down our denunciations of sin lest we be accused of being "judgmental"; we minimize doctrinal distinctives lest we be accused of being "divisive"; we blur the boundaries between virtue

and vice lest we be accused of being "legalistic"; we brush off
heresy and heterodoxy lest we be accused of being "intolerant";
and we veil our concerns about societal disarray lest we be accused
of being "political."

Indeed, the well-polished civility of our religious talk has all but
eliminated true religion from our talk—to say nothing of our lives.
Thus, recovery seems to have replaced repentance; dysfunction
seems to have replaced sin; drama seems to have replaced dogma;
positive thinking seems to have replaced passionate preaching;
subjective experience seems to have replaced propositional truth; a
practical regimen seems to have replaced a providential redemption; psychotherapy seems to have replaced discipleship;
encounter groups seem to have replaced evangelistic teams; the
don't-worry-be-happy jingle seems to have replaced the prepare-
to-meet-thy-God refrain; the Twelve Steps seem to have replaced
the One Way.

Today it is far better to be witty than to be weighty. We want
soft-sell. We want relevance. We want acceptance. We want an upbeat, low-key, clever, motivational, friendly, informal, yuppiefied,
and abbreviated faith. No ranting; no raving; no Bible-thumping;
no heavy commitments; no strings attached. No muss; no fuss. We
want the same salvation as in the Old Time Religion—but with
half the hassle and a third less guilt.

Thus, our public services have become little more than entertainment extravaganzas. Pragmatic methodology has all but dis-
placed dogmatic theology. Christian publishing now emphasizes
self-improvement or private diversion and only rarely concentrates
on theological or biblical studies. Ministry has become a con-
sumer-driven commodity—determined by a demographic study, a
niche-group analysis, or a market focus survey—all in an attempt
to attract the baby-boomer, the channel-surfer, and the media-
savvy unbeliever.

In our haste to present the Gospel in this kind of fresh, innovative, and user-friendly fashion, we have come dangerously close to
denying its essentials altogether. We have made it so accessible
that it is no longer biblical. When Karl Barth published his liberal
manifesto *Romerbrief* in 1918, it was said that he had "exploded a
bomb on the playground of theologians."[4] But the havoc brought
about by the current spate of evangelical compromise may well

prove to be far more devastating.

Predictably, the erosion of the distinctiveness of the Gospel has wrought an avalanche of decadence. The moral practices of the average Christian today are not discernibly different from the average non-Christian.[5] It doesn't take a rocket scientist or a social ethicist to figure out that does not bode well for us. What we do or don't do, how we act or don't act, what we want or don't want, are all likely to be practically identical to what our unbelieving neighbors do, act, or want.

Michael Scott Horton asserts that this woeful state of affairs is due to our attempt to "domesticate God."[6] Gary DeMar and Peter Leithart assert it is attributable to the fact that we have succumbed to the "reduction of Christianity."[7] John MacArthur simply says it is because we are "ashamed of the Gospel."[8]

Whatever the cause, it is clear that compromise is now the modern church's most damning dilemma. Theologian Howard Snyder has said:

> Worldliness is the greatest threat to the church today. In other ages the church suffered from dead orthodoxy, live heresy, flight from the world, and other maladies. But the painful truth today is that the church is guilty of massive accommodation to the world.[9]

The Bible says that we are to "come out" from the world (2 Corinthians 6:17). Instead, though, it seems we have done our utmost to blend in. By all appearances we have endeavored to be completely accepted. The Bible says that such carnality is at odds with true spirituality, but we seem to have placed our confident new carnality on a par with spirituality.

And worst of all, most of us never even noticed.

The worldliness of the modern church is thus not really a matter of hypocrisy. Rather, it is something far more insidious. Ethicist Peter Kreeft writes:

> A prominent Christian businessman is exposed as a crook and a bigamist. A historic Christian denomination goes on record as favoring a woman's right to abortion. The second fact is even more shocking than the first. Why? A brilliant Christian writer and pastor leaves his wife and children and runs off with another woman. Then he writes a book justifying it. The second fact is more shocking than the first. Why? Nearly as many of the marriages of

> Christians end in divorce as those of non-Christians. Most
> Christian denominations permit divorce, though Christ did not.
> The second fact is more shocking than the first. Why?

He answers the question:

> In each of these cases, the first statement shows only the perennial
> fact of hypocrisy, of not practicing what one preaches. But the sec-
> ond statements are something altogether new. They represent a
> changing of the rules that makes hypocrisy impossible. The first
> set of facts shows a lack of virtue; the second shows a lack of
> knowledge of virtue. Christians, like other sinners, have always
> been susceptible to vice, but today we no longer seem to know
> what vice and virtue are.

All the towering materialism of modern evangelicalism rests on
one assumption—a false assumption. It is that substantive spirituality can be had apart from disciplined maturity and diligent labor.
The fact is, the compromise of the church is not so much rooted in
a revolt against sexual mores, or against financial scruples, or
against gender roles, or against spiritual integrity. It is instead rooted in the infantilization of the faith. It is rooted in the easing-up of
the demands of the Gospel. It is rooted in the under-estimation of
discipleship. It is rooted in an aversion to work, perseverance, and
holy patience. It is rooted in a revolt against maturity.

Mercy ministry is a function of diligence, faithfulness, and
maturity. It does not survive in an environment of childish compromise. Thus, the modern church's revolt against maturity has all
but eliminated works of compassion from our lives.

Compromise

Though a member of the despised Jewish exile community, the
prophet Daniel had risen to a place of great power and influence in
Babylonian politics and cultures as a fairly young man. Not surprisingly, he attracted the jealous attentions of many within the
empire's cut-throat governing elite:

> The administrators and the satraps tried to find grounds for
> charges against Daniel in his conduct of government affairs, but
> they were unable to do so. They could find no corruption in him,
> because he was trustworthy and neither corrupt nor negligent.

> Finally these men said, "We will never find any basis for charges
> against this man Daniel unless it has something to do with the law
> of his God." (Daniel 6:4–5)

Appealing to the king's vanity, the rulers were able to encourage
him to sign the decree: No person could pray or ask anything of
any man but the king for thirty days. If someone defied the law?
He would be thrown to a den full of hungry lions.

Daniel was a man of principle. He was a man of conviction. He
refused to be drawn into the petty world of politics. He was a wise
man who simply would not sacrifice integrity for pragmatism.

He had been providentially raised up to a position of tremendous cultural influence by the Lord God, and so he owed his first
allegiance to Him. He would not, and he could not, compromise
that commitment. God's will, God's purpose, and God's agenda for
his life were completely non-negotiable as far as he was concerned:

> Now when Daniel learned that the decree had been published, he
> went home to his upstairs room where the windows opened
> toward Jerusalem. Three times a day he got down on his knees and
> prayed, giving thanks to his God, just as he had done before.
> (Daniel 6:10)

Daniel refused to yield to the pressure of the world. That did
not mean that he was inflexible, archaic, and moss-backed. On the
contrary, he was remarkably creative (Daniel 1:12–13). He was
capable and discerning (1:4). He was learned and had understanding (1:20). He was dedicated and teachable (1:17). He was selfless
and discreet (2:14–18). His extraordinary wisdom and insight won
for him the audience of earthly kings (5:13–14), and his extraordinary piety and devotion won for him the audience of heavenly
hosts (9:3–22). He was highly esteemed by men, by angels, and by
God.

Still, his unswerving commitment and his righteous determination were inimitable. He was forthright in his condemnation of sin.
He was unguarded in his pronouncement of truth. He was single-
minded in his adherence to the Word of God and the worship of
God.

Daniel obeyed the clear command of Scripture to be steadfast
and unwavering.

A stand like that can be costly, though, and it nearly cost Daniel everything.

Think of it. He had power. He had influence. He had prominence. But he risked it all for the sake of conscience. A simple compromise anywhere along the way would have preserved his power, influence, and prominence. But he refused to compromise.

He could have tried to work within the system. He could have tried to wait out the edict. He wouldn't have had to deny his faith, just keep it quiet for a little while. He could have tried conciliation, accommodation, or negotiation. Why waste everything that he had gained over such a small matter? Why not just play along, attempting to do good as the opportunity presented itself?

Truth always invites opposition. There is no way around it.

But no. Not for Daniel. He refused to compromise—risking prison and even death. He refused for three reasons.

First, Daniel understood who really governs men and nations. He did not need to tremble before mere human edicts. God and God alone directs the ebb and flow of history: "The king's heart is in the hand of the Lord; he directs it like a watercourse wherever he pleases" (Proverbs 21:1).

Daniel knew that the resolution of any power, influence, or prominence that he might have had depended upon God's sovereign purpose. His only responsibility was his own personal covenantal loyalty and obedience.

Daniel knew that the outcome of all events lay in providence—which was thankfully beyond his purview or control. Compromise was out of the question. Thus, he could rest in the Lord's wisdom and concentrate on simply doing his job.

Second, Daniel understood the nature of his opposition. He knew that his enemies would not be satisfied with anything less than the assassination of his faith and the obliteration of his privilege. Compromise would have been fruitless. It wouldn't have accomplished anything more than a watering down of his message.

He knew that the truth always invites opposition. There is no way around it. No amount of compromise can divert it.

Persecution is inevitable.

Thus, no matter what concessions or accommodations Daniel would have made, his enemies would have continued their assaults against him. Compromise would have done little more than buy some time.

Third, Daniel understood the fundamental truth that God is able to make seemingly negative circumstances work together for good for His people. By refusing to compromise, he knew that he was risking prison or death. But he also knew that the threat of both prison and death could easily become marvelous opportunities under the sovereign direction of God Almighty.

The testimony of Scripture in this matter is clear:

- Like Daniel, Joseph risked everything by refusing to compromise his obedience to God (Genesis 39:7–16). As a result, he was thrown into prison (Genesis 39:19–20). But God used that prison experience as the first stage of his ultimate victory. Before long, Joseph was raised up out of the depths to exercise authority over the whole land (Genesis 41:37–45).

- Similarly, David risked everything by refusing to compromise his obedience to God (1 Samuel 18:1–16). As a result, he was cast into exile (1 Samuel 19:11–18). But God used the experience of exile as the first stage of his ultimate victory. Before long, David was raised up out of the depths to exercise authority over the whole land (2 Samuel 2:4).

- The early Christians also risked everything by refusing to compromise their obedience to God (Acts 4:19–20). As a result, they were thrown into prison (Acts 5:18). But God used that prison experience as the first stage of their ultimate victory. Before long they were raised up out of the depths to exercise authority over the whole land (Acts 5:19; 19:26).

Like Daniel, many heroes of the faith witnessed the resurrection power of Almighty God. Esther, Job, Elijah, Hosea, and the apostle Paul each saw the most difficult and oppressive circumstances providentially transformed into glorious victory.[10] Each of them went from death to life, from bondage to liberty, from prison to promise. All of them mirrored and illuminated in their lives and experiences the outline of the Gospel of grace.

Jesus refused to compromise His message and mission, of course. As a result, He was thrown into the prison of the grave. But God used that prison experience as the first stage of His ultimate victory. On the third day Jesus arose out of the depths to exercise authority—to rule and reign—over the whole world. This is the essence of the salvific work.

So, Daniel's uncompromising stand was rooted in his understanding of God's sovereignty and man's opposition. But it was also rooted in his comprehension of the privilege of prison and the promise of resurrection. He could remain steadfast because he was wise enough to recognize that the trials in his own experience were designed to forge a new level of maturity in his life and to lay the foundations of some future victory. He could therefore "live by faith, not by sight" (2 Corinthians 5:7).

Steadfastness

An uncompromising stance before the watching world is all too often mistaken for prideful self-assurance. Because he understood who really governs men and nations, because he understood the nature of his opposition, and because he understood that God would transform prison into promise, Daniel refused to hedge God's statutes. His enemies took this to be mere hardheaded stubbornness (Daniel 6:13). They presumed that Daniel was just another in a long line of self-confident, egotistical, and dogmatic men.

Uncompromising steadfastness is almost always confused with unreasonableness. Righteousness is thus inevitably labeled "intolerant," "judgmental," and "biased." Righteous men and women are always popularly diagnosed as "suffering from delusions of grandeur."

But nothing could be further from the truth.

Uncompromising believers throughout the ages who have "conquered kingdoms, administered justice, and gained what was promised; who shut the mouths of lions, quenched the fury of the flames, and escaped the edge of the sword; whose weakness was turned to strength" did so "by faith" (Hebrews 11:33–34). In other words, they trusted God rather than themselves. Far from having confidence or certainty in their own flesh, their own ideas, their own understanding, their own abilities, their own strength, and their own ingenuity, they put their full reliance on God (Philippians 3:3). They obtained victory even amidst great difficulty, not because they were domineering and proud, but because they were submissive to continue in the tasks placed before them, because they yielded humbly to their peculiar calling.

The Bible is crystal clear in this matter:

> Be still before the Lord and wait patiently for him; do not fret when men succeed in their ways, when they carry out their wicked schemes. Refrain from anger and turn from wrath; do not fret—it leads only to evil. For evil men will be cut off, but those who hope in the Lord will inherit the land. A little while, and the wicked will be no more; though you look for them, they will not be found. But the meek will inherit the land and enjoy great peace. (Psalm 37:7–11).

Notice that in times of travail or persecution, believers are to bear up under the strain simply by continuing in their regular work of merciful service. They are to carry on by meeting the needs of others. God gives no special trick to avoiding the pitfalls of compromise. There is no gimmick of spiritual whoop-tee-doo warfare. It does not require a steely resolve or an iron will. It is instead found in a mature and contented attention to the details of our daily labor and our common calling.

The enemies of the Gospel often mistake this single-minded dedication to the work at hand as a kind of prideful know-it-all aloofness. That many Christians today make the same mistake is a telling commentary on the modern evangelical mind-set.[11]

Work

We may not like to admit it, but work is the heart and soul, the cornerstone, of man's created purpose. It is the basis of all ministry, and it is the foundation upon which true compassion is built. God's first word to man was definitive:

> Be fruitful and increase in number; fill the earth and subdue it. Rule over the fish of the sea and the birds of the air and over every living creature that moves on the ground. (Genesis 1:28).

In other words: *work.*

The Bible is replete with teaching on work. But its basic thrust may be reduced to four basic points:

First, the Bible teaches that all honorable work is holy.

Far from being a bitter consequence of the Fall, work is a vital aspect of God's overall purpose for man in space and time. For that reason, He has typically used workmen, ordinary laborers, in the enactment of that purpose. He has used shepherds like Jacob and David. He has used farmers like Amos and Gideon. He has used merchants like Abraham and Lydia. He has used craftsmen like Aquilla and Paul. He has used artists like Solomon and Bezalel. And the men He chose to revolutionize the Roman Empire in the first century were a motley band of fishermen and tax collectors.

The Fourth Commandment, though commonly and correctly understood as prohibition against working on the Sabbath, has another all-too-often neglected injunction: "Six days you shall labor and do all your work" (Exodus 20:9).

Second, the Bible teaches that God calls each person to his or her work:

> There are different kinds of gifts, but the same Spirit. There are different kinds of service, but the same Lord. There are different kinds of working, but the same God works all of them in all men. (1 Corinthians 12:4–6)

The doctrine of calling was once the distinctive principle of the Reformation. And rightly so. Cotton Mather, the great American colonial preacher, wrote:

> A Christian should follow his occupation with contentment. Is your business here clogged with any difficulties and inconveniences? Contentment under those difficulties is no little part of your homage to that King who hath Placed you where you are by His call.[12]

Third, the Bible teaches that work is intended for the benefit of the community. It is not just to benefit ourselves. By work, we are to uphold our responsibility to provide for our family (1 Timothy 5:8), build the work of Christ's kingdom, and share with those in need (Ephesians 4:28). Work is mercy. It is service.

Fourth, the Bible teaches that, because of sin's devastation, the high ideals of the work-ethic can be attained only through Christ's restoration, imparted to us in the Gospel.

The Fall has disrupted and obstructed the blessings of work. Man cannot, and will not, work as he should (Genesis 3:17–19). Sin blinds, and binds us, so that our divine commission is left unfulfilled.

In a very real sense, everything that the Bible teaches about the benefits of work can stand only as a condemnation to fallen man. Such things as poverty and privation in our midst are but standing reminders of this fact.

Thanks be to God, in Jesus Christ we are restored. In Him, our lives and our work are redeemed from futility and made meaningful once again.

Whenever the peculiar people of God have tended to their work and left the outcome of external events to the care of providence, they have successfully resisted the temptation to compromise. Like Daniel, when they have simply fulfilled their calling and done their jobs, they have been able to avoid accommodation with the world. And they have been able to fulfill their calling as agents of mercy in this poor fallen world.

Beyond the Wicket Gate

Next to the Bible, the best-loved and most-read book during the first three hundred years of American colonial and national life was John Bunyan's *Pilgrim's Progress.* Its plot was familiar to every schoolchild. Its characters became cultural icons. Its imagery was woven into the art, music, literature, and ideas of the people.

The opening lines of the saga were etched into the memories of untold thousands of people and became a kind of yardstick against which to measure literary and devotional excellence:

> As I walked through the wilderness of this world, I lighted on a certain place where was a den, and I laid me down in that place to sleep, and as I slept I dreamed a dream. I dreamed, and behold I saw a man clothed in rags, standing in a certain place, with his face from his own house, a book in his hand, and a great burden on his back. I looked and saw him open the book, and read therein; and as he read he wept and trembled, and not being able longer to contain, he brake out with a lamentable cry, saying: What shall I do?[13]

First published in 1678, the vivid allegory detailed the trials and tribulations of a young man named Pilgrim (later in the text changed to Christian) as he made his way through the treacherous world. He was a pilgrim—journeying toward his ultimate home, the Celestial City. Along the way he passed through such tempestuous places as Vanity Fair, the Slough of Despond, Strait Gate, the Hill of Difficulty, Delectable Mountains, By-Path Meadow, Doubting Castle, and Mount Caution. Those inhospitable locales were populated by a variety of carefully-drawn villains such as Obstinate, Pliable, Mr. Worldly-Wiseman, Mistrust, Timorous, Wanton, Talkative, Envy, Mr. Money-Love, Faint-Heart, and Little-Faith. Despite the fact that he was helped from time to time by a whole host of heroic characters such as Evangelist, Faithful, Good Will, Hopeful, Knowledge, Experience, Watchful, and Sincere, the hapless pilgrim had to struggle through one difficulty or distraction after another. Again and again he was forced to decide between compromise or faithfulness, between accommodation with the world or holy perseverance, between the wide way to destruction or the narrow road to glory.

After overcoming a number of chilling risks and hazards, the story was ultimately resolved—like virtually all great classic works of literature—with a happy ending.

Though written in a coarse, speech-patterned prose—a far cry from the polite literary convention of the seventeenth century—the book was almost immediately acclaimed as a masterpiece of imagination and inspiration. Even those Christians who chafed a bit at Bunyan's Puritan theology, his Calvinistic doctrine, and his non-conformist practice readily identified with his beautifully realized vision of life in this fallen world. What appeared on the surface to be little more than a series of adventures or a blithe narrative of folk-tale ups and downs, was, in fact, a penetrating portrayal of the universal human experience.

Pilgrim's Progress struck a nerve.

The reason was simple enough: The question of compromise nags at all of us. The pressure to accommodate ourselves to the pattern of this world is an almost omnipresent and ubiquitous dilemma. It is no less real to the banker in New York, the grocer in Kansas City, the sales clerk in Houston, the professor in San Diego, the housewife in Seattle, or the restaurateur in Toronto than it was to Christian in the Wicket-Gate.

Bunyan knew this only too well—from painful personal experience. As the pastor of a small separatist congregation during a time of fierce persecution, he was repeatedly flogged and imprisoned for his faith. Once he spent nearly twelve years in Bedford's little jail perched over the River Ouse. At any time he could have ensured his release—if he would only promise not to preach without approval or license.

All he had to do was to compromise his principles, and he could have been reunited with his impoverished wife and children. All he had to do was to accommodate himself to the realities of life under the restored Stuart monarchy, and he could have continued with a full—albeit quiet—ministry among his neighbors. All he had to do was to renounce his peculiar bias, his odd methods, his curious lifestyle. All he had to do was to fit in.

Though his resolve undoubtedly wavered from time to time, in the end he remained steadfast. Like Christian, he persevered.

It was during those tortured years of confinement that Bunyan wrote his allegorical story. Drawing from obvious autobiographical details, he threw the searchlight of understanding on the soul of Everyman.

As literary critic Roger Sharrock said: "A seventeenth-century Calvinist sat down to write a tract and produced a folk-epic of the universal religious imagination instead."[14]

In our own day, when compromise is more prevalent than ever before, Bunyan's classic is perhaps more relevant than ever before.

Done With

In his final message to the church in the twentieth century, Francis Schaeffer bemoaned evangelicalism's flight from work and its consequent immature accommodation to the world:

> Have we as evangelicals been on the front lines contending for the faith and confronting the moral breakdown over the last forty to sixty years? Have we even been aware that there is a battle going on—not just a heavenly battle, but a life and death struggle over what will happen to men and women and children in both this life and the next? If the truth of the Christian faith is in fact truth, then it stands in antithesis to the ideas and immorality of our age, and it

must be practiced in both teaching and practical action. Truth demands confrontation. It must be loving confrontation, but it must be confrontation nonetheless. Sadly we must say that this has seldom happened. Most of the evangelical world has not been active in the battle, or even been able to see that we are in a battle. And when it comes to the issues of the day the evangelical world most often has said nothing; or worse has said nothing different from what the world would say. Here is the great evangelical disaster—the failure of the evangelical world to stand for truth as truth. There is only one word for this—namely accommodation: the evangelical church has accommodated itself to the spirit of the age.[15]

Similarly, Martin Luther asserted:

If I profess with the loudest voice and clearest exposition every portion of the truth of God except precisely that little point which the world and the devil are at the moment attacking, I am not confessing Christ, however boldly I may be professing Christ. Where the battle rages, there the loyalty of the soldier is proved and to be steady on all the battle front besides, is mere flight and disgrace if he flinches at that point.[16]

The prophet Micah reminded the people of his day that this kind of simple and balanced attentiveness to the work at hand was the most merciful approach to the smothering conformity of the world and the best antidote to the withering accommodation of the world (Micah 4:4–5). Though such a lifestyle is a rebuke to the world (Micah 4:3), it is nevertheless ultimately quite alluring and enticing (Micah 4:1–2). Thus the Micah Mandate affords us the resources to maintain our peculiarity before a watching world.

John Bunyan knew that only too well.

In the center of Bedford, England, stands a statue of Bunyan carrying a tinker's burden upon his back and a Bible in his hand. It marks the place where that great Puritan spent the long years of his imprisonment for the offense of teaching and preaching without proper state certification. Near the foot of the statue is a little bronze plaque. On it are engraved the words of the prosecutor—the Lord Judge Magistrate of Bedford—spoken at Bunyan's sentencing in 1673. The judge said:

At last we are done with this tinker and his cause. Never more will he plague us: for his name, locked away as surely as he, shall be forgotten, as surely as he. Done we are, and all eternity with him.[17]

Of course, it is not Bunyan who is forgotten. Instead, it is the Lord Judge Magistrate of Bedford who remains unnamed and unremembered. Bunyan foiled the plans of the powers and the principalities by holding fast to that which was once and for all delivered unto the saints: a world-and-life view rooted in the grace of a sovereign God and the uncompromised maturity of diligence in daily work.

MERCY WORK

"He has showed you, O man, what is good. And what does the Lord require of you? To act justly and to love mercy and to walk humbly with your God"
(*Micah* 6:8).

Mercy ministry has always been the primary work of Christians in the world—serving as the conduit for evangelism, pastoral care, and cultural influence. From the beginning, the heroes of the faith have been those who have at great risk refused to compromise with the world and instead worked hard to show forth mercy and compassion. Examples abound:

Alban of Verlamium (154–91) is widely venerated as the first Christian martyr on the Island of Britain. During the last few decades of the second century he offered refuge to those fleeing the persecution against the church. He succored the sick, cared for the poor, and saved abandoned children from certain death. Bede the historian records his brutal martyrdom on Holmhurst Hill after he tried to intercede on behalf of a pitiful family of refugees. Though his work in the world was brief, his uncompromising commitment to mercy continues to inspire the faithful to fulfill their callings regardless of the opposition they may face.

When *Hugh Goldie* (1706–1881) joined a mission station in Old Calabar on the West Coast of Africa early in the nineteenth century, he was horrified by many of the things he found there. The living conditions of the people were utterly deplorable. Their nutrition was abominable. Their hygiene was disgraceful. Their social and commercial arrangements were in utter disarray. But it was their cavalier attitude to the sanctity of human life that most disturbed him. Although they had recently abandoned the centuries-old practice of human sacrifice, they still freely practiced abortion, abandonment, and infanticide. Though Goldie was met with stiff opposition by the tribal chiefs—and even by many of his fellow missionaries who felt that his pro-life convictions would compromise their evangelistic efforts—he stood firmly on the integrity of the whole counsel of God. Finally, as a result of his life-long crusade for life, tribal decrees in 1851 and 1878 banned the terrible customs. He went on to his eternal reward having "fought the good fight," "finished the race," and "kept the faith" (2 Timothy 4:7).

Joseph Damien de Veuster (1840–89) grew up in the lowlands of Belgium. After posting a promising academic record, he disappointed his family's expectations of a brilliant professional career in business, law, or politics by submitting to a call to the mission field. Assigned to the newly reopened islands of Hawaii, he served as a pastor in the burgeoning village of Honolulu for nearly a decade. His concern for the sanctity of all human life led him not only to fight against the few remaining abortionists among the natives, but to eventually request a transfer to the wretched leprosarium on Molakai. There, Damien helped the people to build homes, schools, roads, civic halls, and treatment clinics. He protected the integrity of each resident from persecution and rejection—both from within and without the colony. Encouraging the essential Christian values of faith, family, and work, he helped restore dignity, hope, and purpose to the despised and rejected. His sacrificial character was soon lauded around the globe. Even the renowned literary skeptic, Robert Louis Stevenson, was struck by Damien's saintly service to the unwanted; Stevenson actually risked his fortune and his reputation by publishing a defense of the great man. Eventually contracting leprosy himself, Damien died at the age of forty-nine. On his tombstone were engraved the words, "Died a Martyr of Charity."

Dozens of others could be cited throughout the wide span of history: Barlaam of Antioch (d. 327), Dunstan of Canterbury (d. 988), Cajetan Gaetano (d. 1547), Zephaniah Swift (d. 1834), Anna Bowden (d. 1844), Lemuel Whitman (d. 1846), and Booker T. Washington (d. 1915). Each buckled down to the tasks at hand in this poor fallen world: demonstrating obedience to Christ, mercy to the afflicted, and diligence despite opposition.

TOUGH AND TENDER MERCIES

*"He has showed you, O man, what is good.
And what does the Lord require of you? To act
justly and to love mercy and to walk humbly
with your God" (Micah 6:8).*

Have you ever noticed how work and mercy are connected throughout the Bible? Do a quick topical study of the way that diligence in our calling leads to effective service and compassion. A Bible dictionary is a good place to start—but you might also want to simply follow the marginal references in a study Bible.

Think about the unexpected opportunities God has afforded you to do acts of mercy while on the job, while exercising your calling, or while developing your gifts. Make a list of the ways you think you might be able to be used sometime in the future.

What do you want to be doing and where do you want to be in two years? In five years? In ten years? How do your dreams coincide with your calling? And how do they together relate to your past opportunities to live mercifully and compassionately?

Different seasons of life provide different opportunities to use our gifts, our callings, and our vocations to serve others. What should you be doing at this particular time in your life? Now, just do it.

Notes

1. *Walt Kelley's Pogo Letter,* Spring 1994.

2. Kenneth Meyers, *All God's Children Wear Blue Suede Shoes* (Wheaton, Ill.: Crossway, 1989), xi.

3. Neil Postman, *Amusing Ourselves to Death* (New York: Penguin, 1985), 115.

4. John Gerstner, *Wrongly Dividing the Word of Truth* (Brentwood, Tenn.: Wolgemuth and Hyatt, 1991), ix.

5. George Barna, *The Frog in the Kettle* (Ventura, Calif.: Regal, 1990), 7.

6. *The Horse's Mouth,* April 1994.

7. Gary DeMar and Peter Leithart, *The Reduction of Christianity* (Atlanta, Ga.: American Vision, 1988).

8. John MacArthur, *Ashamed of the Gospel* (Wheaton, Ill.: Crossway, 1993).

9. John White, *Flirting with the World* (Wheaton, Ill.: Harold Shaw, 1982), 9.

10. Esther (Esther 3:6–15; 8:1–17), Job (Job 1:13–22; 42:10–15), Elijah (1 Kings 17:1–16; 18:20–46), Hosea (Hosea 1:2–9; 3:1–5), and the apostle Paul (Philippians 3:8–16).

11. *World,* 7 May 1994.

12. Hyksos Pappas, *Cotton Mather* (New York: Athena, 1926), 67.

13. John Bunyan, *Pilgrim's Progress* (New York: Penguin, 1965), 51.

14. Ibid., 27.

15. Francis Schaeffer, *The Great Evangelical Disaster* (Wheaton, Ill.: Crossway, 1983), 37.

16. Ibid., 51.

17. *Tennessee Education Review,* July 1993.

HUMILITY:
TO DO WELL

*Everyone should consider himself as entrusted
not only with his own conduct, but with that
of others; and as accountable, not only for
the duties he neglects or the crimes which he
commits, but for the negligence and
irregularity which he may encourage or inculcate.*
Samuel Johnson

OUR CODEPENDENT LOVE

*Like peace, regeneration carries a price which
those who think of it idly will balk at.*
Richard Weaver

T he *Westminster Confession of Faith* was written between 1643 and 1648 by a remarkable group of English reformers. The cornerstone of its magnificent formulation of biblical orthodoxy is its conception of God's nature and character:

> There is but one only living and true God, who is infinite in being and perfection, a most pure spirit, invisible, without body, parts, or passions, immutable, immense, eternal, incomprehensible, almighty; most wise, most holy, most free, most absolute, working all things according to the counsel of His own immutable and most righteous will, for His own glory; most loving, gracious, merciful, long-suffering, abundant in goodness and truth, forgiving iniquity, transgression and sin; the rewarder of them that diligently seek Him; and withal most just and terrible in His judgments; hating all sin, and who will by no means clear the guilty.[1]

The *Confession* concludes with a practical admonition: "To Him is due from angels and men, and every other creature, whatsoever worship, service, or obedience He is pleased to require of them."[2]

Though such an understanding of God formed the backdrop of the thinking of people in the early days of this country—and thus, in turn, much of the fabric of early American culture—it is a far

cry from our own comprehension of God today. In fact, the doctrinal precision of the Westminster divines sounds rather foreign to
our ears, not just because they used an exacting tone and a majestic language at odds with our relaxed syntax and simple prose, but
because their very perception of God is foreign to us.

We are prone to think of God—when we think of Him at all—
as wonderful. We are less likely to see Him as deliberate. Certainly
He is both, but the overwhelming emphasis of Scripture is upon
the will rather than the wonder. It is upon the exercise of God's
prerogative rather than the satisfaction of our pleasure. The difference is probably a matter of slights rather than slanders.
Nevertheless, it is a difference that makes for rather dramatic consequences.

Thus, to some of us God is little more than a cosmic vending
machine in the sky, designed to dispense our every want and
whim. To others of us He is a grandfatherly sage who lives to
patiently offer us certain therapeutic benefits and baubles from His
largess. To still others He is a kind of Santa figure—jolly, unflappable, and determined to bestow goodies upon all mankind.
Invariably, though, we moderns tend to see God in terms of ourselves—in terms of our wants, our needs, our preferences, and our
desires. We have apparently, as Voltaire accused, "made God in our
own image."[3]

To the Westminster divines, such a conception of God would
have been altogether unrecognizable as the God of the Bible. Such
a conception would have been incapable of laying foundations for
a theology of balance—thus rendering the flowering of American
civilization utterly impossible.

In fact, according to psychologist Paul Vitz, such a conception
is not knowledge of God at all, but a form of "self-worship."[4] Thus,
according to D. Martyn Lloyd-Jones, "because men do not know
God or the nature of God—particularly those who claim to be
Christians—all of the problems of life and culture are amplified
even more."[5] Andrew Murray asserts that it is due to the fact that
Christians do not "properly entertain a knowledge of God" that
"societies fall into such disarray as we have in the modern world."[6]
And A. W. Tozer has said that "a lack of a true knowledge of God's
attributes and character" is the "root of the indecisiveness, imbalance, and ineffectiveness" of the contemporary church.[7]

That is a tragedy in more ways than one. J. I. Packer, in his devotional masterpiece, *Knowing God*, has said:

> What were we made for? To know God. What aim should we set ourselves in life? To know God. What is the "eternal life" that Jesus gives? Knowledge of God. What is the best thing in life, bringing more joy, delight, and contentment, than anything else? Knowledge of God. What, of all the states God ever sees man in, gives Him most pleasure? Knowledge of Himself.[8]

Thus, if we fail to come to a full and accurate knowledge of God—if it is shallow, or superficial, or self-centered as our modern evangelical conception of God is apt to be—then we are not only likely to miss God's purpose and will for our lives, we are likely to make a mess of the world around us as well.

And so we have.

The Earth Is the Lord's

Nebuchadnezzar, the great king of the Babylonian empire during the sixth century before Christ, might sympathize. As he walked about his splendid palace one day, he voiced his thoughts about his self-worth: "Is not this the great Babylon I have built as the royal residence, by my mighty power and for the glory of my majesty?" (Daniel 4:30). But then, Scripture relates,

> The words were still on his lips when a voice came from heaven, "This is what is decreed for you, King Nebuchadnezzar: Your royal authority has been taken from you. You will be driven away from people and will live with the wild animals; you will eat grass like cattle. Seven times will pass by for you until you acknowledge that the Most High is sovereign over the kingdoms of men and gives them to anyone he wishes." (Daniel 4:31–32)

He was the greatest king of the ancient world. His reign was resplendent with glory, honor, and power. The city he built was magnificent, unrivaled in its scope and vision. The empire he assembled was mythically proportioned, unrivaled in its strength and valor. The reputation that he forged was universal, unrivaled in its supremacy and vastness. And yet, Nebuchadnezzar was still but a man.

He thought he was something more. He imagined for himself a majesty that transcended that of all other men. He reveled in the storehouse of his great pride. He boasted of his invincibility.

And so, God humbled him. He decreed that Nebuchadnezzar would be reminded of the frailty of human flesh. He decreed that the great king would be forced to acknowledge a King greater still:

> Immediately what had been said about Nebuchadnezzar was fulfilled. He was driven away from people and ate grass like cattle. His body was drenched with the dew of heaven until his hair grew like the feathers of an eagle and his nails like the claws of a bird. (Daniel 4:33)

The quick demotion of Nebuchadnezzar was a vivid demonstration to all the citizens of Babylon that God alone is sovereign and almighty, that God alone is to be exalted and praised, that God alone is the possessor of all greatness, power, glory, and majesty in heaven and on earth.

The lesson was not lost on the king or his subjects:

> At the end of that time, I, Nebuchadnezzar, raised my eyes toward heaven, and my sanity was restored. Then I praised the Most High; I honored and glorified him who lives forever. His dominion is an eternal dominion; his kingdom endures from generation to generation. All the peoples of the earth are regarded as nothing. He does as he pleases with the powers of heaven and the peoples of the earth. (Daniel 4:34–35)

When he finally realized the truth, Nebuchadnezzar was restored to his kingdom. This time he had learned his lesson. He says it clearly: "Now I, Nebuchadnezzar, praise and exalt and glorify the King of heaven, because everything he does is right and all his ways are just. And all those who walk in pride he is able to humble" (Daniel 4:37).

Nebuchadnezzar learned the most central truth in all the cosmos: God sovereignly rules over all things. He learned that God and God alone is supreme, that God is the "King of kings and Lord of lords."

God sovereignly rules because He is the creator and owner and sustainer of all things above and below. Nebuchadnezzar had to learn the hard way that the whole universe is in a very real sense *theocentric/centric*=centered (*theos*=God). It is *theocentric* now. God's central rule of all things is not something we must wait for. It is not something that we must attempt to usher in through the manipulations of the political process or the revolutionary subversion of human governments. It is a reality right this very moment. "Hallelujah! For our Lord God Almighty reigns" (Revelation 19:6).

The Bible is absolutely clear on this point. There is nothing in heaven above or on earth below that escapes His jurisdiction. God rules.

God sovereignly rules the forces of creation:

> He sends his command to the earth; his word runs swiftly. He spreads the snow like wool and scatters the frost like ashes. He hurls down his hail like pebbles. Who can withstand his icy blast? He sends forth his word and melts them; he stirs up his breezes, and the waters flow. (Psalm 147:15–18)

God also sovereignly rules the course of history. The ultimate destiny of both men and nations lies in His hands:

> Remember the former things, those of long ago; I am God, and there is no other; I am God, and there is none like me. I have made known the end from the beginning, from ancient times, what is still to come. I say: My purpose will stand, and I will do all that I please. (Isaiah 46:9–10)

God sovereignly rules the hearts and minds and ways of men as well. Though He yields us extraordinary freedoms, we remain under the discretion of His divine purpose and plan:

> In his heart a man plans his course, but the Lord determines his steps. (Proverbs 16:9)

God even sovereignly rules the nations of the earth. He is King over all kings and Lord over all lords:

> The Lord foils the plans of the nations; he thwarts the purposes of the peoples. (Psalm 33:10)

The fact is God rules everything and everyone, everywhere and at all times. He is the one true Master of the universe. Again, this is not something that we have to somehow confirm through political or cultural processes. It is not a temporal objective that we must strive toward. God is even now on the throne.

The Christian Life

Clearly then, the goal of Christian living in the world is not to usher in some new theocratic order or enforce some new theocratic code. It is instead to simply acknowledge the theocentric order that already exists by virtue of the nature and character of God (Proverbs 3:6). It is to know God for who He actually is and to live accordingly. It is to "glorify God and to enjoy Him forever."[9]

> ## Most of us . . . are so self-centered and self-consumed that we fail to take the nature and character of God into account.

Christian activity in the world therefore is not supposed to attempt an imposition of a messianic kingdom from the top down. Only God can lawfully control the hearts of men by imposing His rule. The balanced Christian life before the watching world is thus merely a public expression of our loyalty to Him and our submission to the Word which reveals Him in His fullness—it is an outward expression of our humility before Almighty God. The daily Christian walk is therefore a bottom-up and inside-out process in the light of our knowledge of God.

The Bible asserts that the administration of the government of God rests on the shoulders of Jesus Christ. It is His robe of glory. The Christian life is simply a recognition of and a submission to that fact. It actively affirms in word and deed that Christ is the creator and sustainer of the universe, that even now He "upholds all things by the Word of His power" (Hebrews 1:3 NASB), and that there will be no end to the increase of His government or of peace. It freely confesses what Nebuchadnezzar was forced to admit: "His dominion is an eternal dominion; his kingdom endures from generation to generation" (Daniel 4:34). The balanced Christian life is nothing more and nothing less than the daily and continuous declaration: "Jesus is Lord"—the most basic of all Christian declarations (Romans 10:9).

Sadly, most of us have repeatedly made Nebuchadnezzar's foolish mistake—we are so self-centered and self-consumed that we fail to take the nature and character of God into account. We have thus been unaware of the fact that Christ bears the ensigns of the theocentricity of heaven and earth: a crown of glory and honor, a sword of truth and justice, a scepter of righteousness and authority, a crest of promise and consolation, and a name of prerogative and transcendence.[10] We have acted as if the lordship of Christ was not the least bit real in terms of the management of our daily schedules and agendas.

We have acted like Nebuchadnezzar.

As a result, we have often, like Nebuchadnezzar, suffered utter humiliation. The enemies of the Gospel scoff and ridicule. They persecute and antagonize. They run roughshod over the weak and helpless. They pollute the land with abomination and desecration. And all the while, we are scuttled the off to the oblivion of irrelevance. All for the lack of the knowledge of God. All for the lack of a simple comprehension of the fact that Christ is the Lord over the totality of life—that God rules.

Of course, Nebuchadnezzar learned his lesson. His humiliation convinced him without a doubt that God "sets up kings and deposes them" (Daniel 2:21); God appoints over the land whomsoever He will; God rules on earth as He does in heaven. Nebuchadnezzar learned his lesson and changed his heart and his life.

What about us?

Fear of God

According to South African theologian and pastor Brendan de Prinster, the clearest evidence that we "have not a true knowledge of God" is that we have ceased to adequately fear Him:

> It is a matter of pride. We have made God into our buddy. We have made Him into our supernatural mascot. We have made Him our co-pilot. Gone is the righteous and royal dread of the Holy One of Israel. Gone is the sense of awe at His Majesty. Gone is the knowledge of His vast power, His unswerving justice, and His uncompromising standards. Gone altogether.[11]

And yet the Bible makes clear that a correct comprehension of God and His attributes will inevitably result in a holy fear of God. Ancient Israel's greatness can be directly attributed to her leaders' fear of God: Abraham was a God-fearer; Joseph was a God-fearer; as were Job, Joshua, David, Jehoshaphat, Hezekiah, Nehemiah, and Jonah.

The balanced Christian life always maintains a twofold expression of holy knowledge and fear: putting a high priority on the centrality of the church and sanctifying whatever time God grants us.

The Church

Though all men are naturally like Nebuchadnezzar: deaf, dumb, and blind to a genuine knowledge of God; though we are bound instead into a selfish covenant with ignorance, defilement, and death; and though we pursue it, choose it, and embrace it, deep down we desire to escape its wretched shackles.

> ## Right doctrine shatters old habits, explodes perverse ideas, and establishes real hope.

Though we may deny it loudly, the truth of God is written on the fleshly tablets of our hearts (Romans 2:14–15). In fact, we must actively restrain or suppress that truth in order to carry on with our destructive ways. Though we deliberately debase ourselves with futile thinking, foolish passions, and filthy behavior, we actually know what is right (Romans 1:19–27). Though we consciously choose the precepts of alienation from God, we cannot escape the awful conviction of the ordinances of intimacy with God.

That is why all men so desperately need the church.

Only the church—as it holds steadfastly to the Word revealed, the Word made manifest, and the Word made alive—is able to effect the kind of comprehensive and reinforced transformation necessary to snap the spell with which sin and ignorance grips each and every one of us—and our society. To the church has been given the command to walk humbly with God and to teach others what it means to do so.

This is due to several great truths:

First, the church renews the minds of fallen men through the teaching and preaching of the Bible—the Word revealed. Right doctrine shatters old habits, explodes perverse ideas, and establishes real hope. The Gospel changes people by the power of the Holy Spirit. Men trapped in the snares of death and darkness need good news. They need the Good News. And thus, God has entrusted the crucial task of publishing that Good News among the nations to the church—and only to the church.

Second, the church readjusts men to genuine life through sacramental worship—the Word made manifest. Worship is not simply an indulgence in abstract theological rituals. Instead, worship is a tangible offering to God, a consecration before God, a communion with God, and a transformation before God. In the simple yet profound act of worship, the meaning and value of life are revealed and fulfilled. It reorients men to God's plan, God's purpose, and God's program (Psalm 73). Once again, God has entrusted this vital function to the church—and only to the church.

Third, the church reforms the lifestyles of men through discipleship—the Word made alive. The disciplined accountability of life in a local church community repatterns believers' ways according to the ways of the Lord. It instills in them godly habits. Through ritual and repetition they are trained to walk in "the course of the just" (Proverbs 2:8) and to avoid "dark ways" (Proverbs 2:13). Through routines of righteousness, they are established in "every good path" (Proverbs 2:9). Thus, people are reformed through the church—and only through the church.

The church has the keys to the Kingdom. It has the power to bind and loose. It has the authority to prevail over the very gates of hell. It offers men the Waters of Life, the Bread of Life, and the Word of Life, because its Head is the Author of Life.

Presbyterian pastor and theologian Peter Leithart in his brilliant book, *The Kingdom and the Power*, makes it clear that in the good providence of God, the church is *Plan A* and there is no *Plan B*. Nevertheless, he says:

> For all the professed religiosity of Americans, comparatively few believe that regular association with a specific group of people is a necessary and central part of a genuinely Christian life. Fewer still think of the church as an institution with real authority over her members; ask any pastor who has tried to enforce discipline, and he will show you his scars.[12]

In contrast, however, he argues that a genuine knowledge and fear of God will ultimately provoke the process of "rediscovering the centrality of the church."[13]

Worship is a tangible offering to God, a consecration before God, a communion with God, and a transformation before God.

Through the ages, the best and the brightest, the kindest and the holiest, have inevitably been those who have walked in awe of Almighty God by making the fellowship, accountability, and ministry of the local church central to their lives and callings.

Time

A genuine knowledge and fear of God will also provoke the process of sanctifying our time as well.

Virtually every biblical injunction about the use of time underlines the importance of each moment that passes. It is an ethical imperative to act and act quickly when lives are at stake, when justice is perverted, when truth is in jeopardy, when mercy is at risk, when souls are endangered, and when the Gospel is assaulted.

We are admonished to make the most of our time (Ephesians 5:15–16). We are to use every day to the utmost. In short, we are to sanctify the time. According to the Bible, our time is not our own. It is not ours to dispose of as we choose. We are to set our days, weeks, and years apart to the Lord for His glory (Romans 14:6–12).

In the Old Testament, days were divided into eight distinct periods: dawn, morning, midday, dark, evening, and three night watches. These were distinguished in the lives of believers by times and seasons of prayer. In the New Testament, the value of this kind of liturgical clock was affirmed by the followers of Christ who punctuated and accentuated their urgent task of evangelization with the discipline of regular spiritual refreshment (Acts 3:1).

Similarly, the weeks of God's people were ordered with purposeful sanctity. In the Old Testament, the week centered around the Sabbath and its attendant sacrifices. In the New Testament, the week revolved around the Lord's Day and the sacraments. Thus, each week had its own pace, its own schedule, its own priorities, and its own order. Thus, believers were able to give form to function and function to form.

Even the years were given special structure and significance to reinforce the biblical conception of decisive urgency. In ancient Israel, feasts, fasts, and festivals paced the community of faith in its progression through the months (Exodus 13:6–10). The early church continued this stewardship of time, punctuating the years with liturgical seasons—Advent, Christmas, Epiphany, Lent, Easter, Ascension, and Pentecost. Thus, God's people were enabled and equipped to run the race, to fight the fight, to finish the course, and to keep the faith.

In order to maintain a sense of balance, it is essential that we maintain the knowledge and fear of God by pacing our efforts through the sanctification of our time. We will thus be able to risk all, remain decisive, and persevere with single-mindedness. We will thus be able to affirm with the psalmist: "My times are in your hands" (Psalm 31:15).

Clearly, there is no room for procrastination or indecision in light of the nature and character of God. We are called to seize the day. Decisiveness, determination, single-mindedness, constancy, diligence, and passion must inform our agenda. The pace we set should be fervent—because the task before us is urgent.

But just as we are to live our lives in holy fear of God with a clear sense of urgency, we are also to measure out that urgency with patience. Victory will not be won in a day, however fervently we act. It will take time—perhaps generations. It has always been that way. It always will be.

In the interim, we are to trust that His sovereign working will indeed make all things right and that His good providence will by no means be thwarted.

Though the times are hard and all the earth cries out under the burden of wickedness, injustice, and perversion, we can relax in the assurance that God is playing the keys of providence according to the score of His own devising. We need not be anxious. We need not worry. We need not fret.

Such is the characteristic of holy patience.

Patience is actually an attribute of God Himself (2 Peter 3:9–15). In addition, it is a command from on high—a non-optional mandate for every believer (Ephesians 4:2). It is a fruit of the Spirit (Galatians 5:22). It is an evidence of love (1 Corinthians 13:4). And it is a qualification for church leadership (2 Timothy 2:24). In times of persecution, suffering, and confrontation, patience is to be the Christian's overriding concern. We are to be patient in hope. We are to be patient in affliction. We are to be patient in our preaching. We are to clothe ourselves in patience. And we are to endure in patience. The pace we set must be steady, because the task we face will not soon be dispatched.

All through the Scriptures this lesson is emphasized.

According to the Bible, we are to imitate others who have manifested a spirit of patience (Hebrews 6:12). Thus, Abraham, Noah, and the apostle Paul are to be our models—as are the legions of other faithful heroes that have gone before us. They faced seemingly insurmountable odds with the calm assurance and the quiet confidence that could only have come from holy patience.

Informed Balance

The grave sin of the people in Micah's day was that they had grown weary of the Lord (Micah 6:3). Obviously, they did not have a proper knowledge of God. Like Nebuchadnezzar they had become prideful, selfish, and decadent. They had become altogether alienated from the truth of God (Micah 6:10–11). They could not even understand the concept of repentance (Micah 6:6–7). And the result was a nation and a culture under judgment (Micah 2:10).

C. S. Lewis has said:

> The essential vice, the utmost evil, is pride. Unchastity, anger, greed, drunkenness, and all that are mere flea-bites in comparison: it was through pride that the devil became the devil; pride leads to every other vice; it is the complete anti-God state of mind.[14]

Christian Dependency

While all the world runs from dependency, the knowledge of God beckons us to humbly welcome it—as we fearfully acknowledge God's sovereign rule and reign in the world and as we yield to the gracious provisions of the church in space and time. Living the balanced Christian life demands it.

Far-Reaching Influence

For several years now I have been a fascinated student of the early years of American life and liberty. Admittedly, separating fact from fiction, exactitude from nostalgia, and history from myth is often more than a little difficult, but I have found it to be well worth the effort. Though I do not hold an idealized perception of that great epoch, I am nevertheless constantly amazed by the breadth and depth of the fledgling American culture and the character of the people who populated it. For us, living in a day when genuine heroes are few and far between—at best—those pioneers provide a startling contrast.

Colonial America produced an extraordinary number of prodigiously gifted men. From William Byrd and George Wythe to Thomas Hutchinson and William Stith, from Robert Beverley and Edward Taylor to Benjamin Franklin and John Bartram, the legacy of the eighteenth-century's native-born geniuses remains unmatched. Their accomplishments—literary, scientific, economic, political, and cultural—are staggering. According to historian Paul Johnson, "Never before has one place and one time given rise to so many great men."[15] As a child, my attentions were naturally drawn to such men as Washington, Hamilton, Adams, Lee, Laurens, Hancock, and the other leaders of the Revolution. But as I have grown older, the men who preceded the so-called founding fathers have captivated my interests. Men like Cotton Mather.

I have often reflected that it is a cruel irony of history that Mather is generally pictured unsympathetically as the archetype of a narrow, intolerant, severe Puritanism, who proved his mettle by prosecuting the Salem witch debacle of 1692. In fact, he never attended the trials—he lived in the distant town of Boston—and actually denounced them. And as for his Puritanism, it was of the most enlightened sort. Mather was a man of vast learning, prodigious talent, and expansive interests. He owned the largest personal library in the New World—consisting of some four thousand volumes ranging across the whole spectrum of classical learning. He was also the most prolific writer of his day, producing some four hundred and fifty books on religion, science, history, philosophy, biography, and poetry. His style ranged from *Magnalia Christi Americana*, dripping with allusions to classical and modern sources, to the practical and straightforward *Essays to Do*

Good, said to be the most influential book ever written in this hemisphere.

He was the pastor of the most prominent church in New England—Boston's North Church. He was active in politics and civic affairs, serving as an adviser to governors, princes, and kings. He taught at Harvard and was instrumental in the establishment of Yale. He was the first native-born American to become a member of the scientific elite in the Royal Society. And he was a pioneer in the universal distribution and inoculation of the smallpox vaccine.

His father, Increase Mather, was the president of Harvard, a gifted writer, a noted pastor, and an influential force in the establishment and maintenance of the second Massachusetts Charter. In his day he was thought to be the most powerful man in New England—in fact, he was elected to represent the colonies before the throne of Charles II in London. But according to many historians, his talents and influence pale in comparison to his son's.

Likewise, both of Cotton Mather's grandfathers were powerful and respected men. His paternal grandfather, Richard Mather, helped draw up the *Cambridge Platform*, which provided a constitutional base for the Congregational churches of New England. And with John Eliot and Thomas Weld, he prepared the *Bay Psalm Book*, which was the first text published in America, achieved worldwide renown, and remains a classic of ecclesiastical literature to this day. His maternal grandfather was John Cotton, who wrote the important Puritan catechism for children, *Milk for Babes*, as well as drawing up the *Charter Template* with John Winthrop as a practical guide for the governance of the new Massachusetts colony. The city of Boston was so named in order to honor him—his former parish work in England was at St. Botolph's Boston.

According to historian George Harper, together these men laid the foundations for a lasting "spiritual dynasty" in America.[16] Even so, according to his lifelong admirer, Benjamin Franklin, "Cotton Mather clearly out-shone them all. Though he was spun from a bright constellation, his light was brighter still."[17]

Mather was assuredly a man of splendid talents and varied interests whose impact covered the whole field of human endeavor, but his greatest contribution may well have been pioneering a theology of biblical balance—one that ultimately gave shape to early American culture and life.

There is no doubt that he was able to combine deep devotion and action into a single and cohesive vision for life and ministry that gave a unique tenor to the American mind-set.[18] He proclaimed a careful balancing of "word and deed, of hand and heart, of the life in the heavenlies and the life of this earth, of personal piety and corporate responsibility."[19]

For Mather this balance was supremely scriptural—drawn from the very nature and character of God. Mather believed there was no alternative but to "yield to every dimension of true discipleship," regardless of the "adjustments of life and comfort" such yielding might bring.[20]

Mather's influence on my own life has been profound. The fact that he could be so active and at the same time so devout impresses me as the very kind of balance that we all ought to strive for. But the fact that this balance was invigorated in his life by an apprehension of God's own character and nature is more impressive still.

Mather wasn't just an overachiever, a pioneer workaholic. He was a man who knew God, disciplined the protocol of his life accordingly, and thereby was used in the good providence of God to alter the destiny of this nation forever.

That is the kind of example I have always desired to follow.

THE CHARACTER ISSUE

"He has showed you, O man, what is good.
And what does the Lord require of you?
To act justly and to love mercy and to
walk humbly with your God" (Micah 6:8).

Through the ages, Christian heroes have demonstrated their fullest comprehension of God's character and attributes as they have humbly centered their lives and ministries in the work of the church in the world. They exercised careful stewardship over the little time they were allotted on this earth to walk in a circumspect fear of the Almighty. Examples abound:

The legendary generosity and charity of *Wenceslas of Bohemia* (907–29) is no mere Christmas fable. The young prince lived a life fraught with conflict and tragedy. Both his mother and grandmother—victims of court intrigue and anti-Christian conspiracy—were murdered when he was young. He himself was the object of several assassination attempts and revolts. Yet, despite such adversity, he was a model Christian regent. He outlawed child abandonment. He criminalized abortion. He reformed the penal system. And he exercised great compassion on the poor. All this because he took seriously the high call of discipleship and a life of service in the church. When he was finally killed by rival heathen elements in the court, his short life was mourned by his subjects and he became for all time the symbol of a holy dependence on a sovereign God.

John Eudes (1570–1649) was born in Normandy at a time when anti-clerical and anti-Christian sentiment there was at a fever pitch. Because his parents remained pious, he tasted the bitter draught of discrimination early in life. Not surprisingly, as an adult he dedicated himself to the care of the persecuted—refugees, the feebleminded, Jews, the sick, Huguenots, and mendicants. He even organized teams of Christian women to care for women reclaimed from prostitution. His fearless and selfless care of the dying distinguished him during two virulent epidemics that swept through France in 1634 and 1639. But it was for his piety before the Lord and his devotion to the church that he was best known. He was unswerving in his commitment to use every moment he had breath to serve his Sovereign.

Louise De Marillac (1626–91) married a high official of the French court and enjoyed a life of privilege and pleasure. Her husband's death left her a widow at the age of thirty-three. That tragedy effected in her a deep desire to serve Christ, and she committed herself to His kingdom. Shortly thereafter, she became a companion and coworker of Vincent De Paul in Paris, caring for the sick and helpless. With him, she launched a sheltering ministry for women in crisis. At the time of her death, the ministry had more than forty houses throughout France and twenty-six more in Paris where abused and exploited women could learn to rebuild their lives. But as with the others, this service was simply the outward expression of an inward commitment to yield every aspect of her life to the ministry of the church and its sovereign King and Savior.

Dozens of others could be cited throughout the wide span of history: Clement of Rome (d. 100), Severinus Boethius (d. 524), Susanna Wesley (d. 1742), Count von Zinzendorf (d. 1760), Howell Harris (d. 1773), Samuel Crowther (d. 1891), and John Mott (d. 1955). Each was committed to serve others through the aegis of the church—not out of a sense of guilt or obligation but out of a solemn recognition of just who God is. And each laid the groundwork for us to live similar lives of submission and obedience.

WITH FEAR AND TREMBLING

*"He has showed you, O man, what is good.
And what does the Lord require of you? To act
justly and to love mercy and to walk humbly
with your God" (Micah 6:8).*

Though we know that the Bible describes the
church as the "royal priesthood" and the "holy
nation" of God's kingdom (1 Peter 2:9), we only
rarely think of it in monarchical terms. Why not do a
study of the way God has established the church
and its ministries as a royal court on this earth?
How would a more regal perspective of God's
monarchical reign affect our vision of the church?
Does our American democratic orientation sometimes cause us to miss key insights about the character of God and the way He desires to walk in this
world?

How central is the life and work of your local church
to you and your family? Do you regularly pray for its
leadership? Do you seek out ways to integrate your
spiritual concerns into its overall outreach? Do you
strive to make your gifts available to its various ministries? What can you do to make the tie that binds
more secure?

Time-management techniques and systems
abound—but they rarely reflect the biblical emphasis of stewardship. Evaluate how you manage your
time—maybe you're fanatical about keeping a daily
planner or maybe you're a little less than organized.
Either way, assess how well your approach facili-
tates your walk with the sovereign Lord. And then
make the changes necessary to bring your days and
seasons under His rule and reign.

Notes

1. *Confession*, II:1–2.

2. Ibid.

3. Thomas Johnson, *The Life and Letters of Benjamin Palmer* (Edinburgh, U.K.: Banner of Truth, 1987), 207.

4. Paul Vitz, *Psychology As Religion: The Cult of Self-Worship* (Grand Rapids: Eerdmans, 1977).

5. *Eklesia*, XX:43.

6. Ibid.

7. Ibid.

8. J. I. Packer, *Knowing God* (Downers Grove, Ill.: InterVarsity, 1973), 29.

9. *Westminster Shorter Catechism*, 1:1.

10. Hebrews 2:9; Revelation 1:16; 2:16; Hebrews 1:8; Revelation 5:5; Philippians 2:9–10.

11. Brendan de Prinster, *The Fear of God* (Johannesburg, S.A.: Kuyperian Tract Society, 1978), 34.

12. Peter Leithart, *The Kingdom and the Power: Recovering the Centrality of the Church* (Phillipsburg, N.J.: P&R, 1993), 142–43.

13. Ibid., iii.

14. C. S. Lewis, *Christian Behavior* (New York: Macmillan, 1943), 44–45.

15. *Eklesia*, XX: 43.

16. *Christian History*, XIII:1.

17. Ibid.

18. Barrett Wendell, *Cotton Mather* (New York: Barnes and Noble, 1992), 154–63.

19. Garland Beecher Ford, *The Early Puritan Synthesis* (Boston: Holliman and Hertz, 1949), 34.

20. Ibid.

JUST DO IT

The whole tendency of modern thought, one might
say its whole moral impulse, is to keep the
individual busy with endless induction.
Richard Weaver

A s is often the case for young aspiring authors, my first attempts at writing took the form of poetry. It was not a promising start. Most of those teenage compositions were rather soppy, maudlin, and sentimental reflections on the shallower things in life. Like the early realms of creation, they were "formless and void."

It wasn't long before I realized that I wasn't getting anywhere writing free verse. So, I decided to try my hand at a few of the more traditional forms of poetry: iambic pentameter, trachaic trimeter, anapestic heptameter, and dactylic dimeter. I wrote quatrains, elegies, odes, idylls, ballads, and sonnets. But it was not until I hit upon the limerick that I found a rhyming scheme that actually suited my utter lack of lyrical discipline—and if the truth be told, my utter lack of lyrical talent. Limericks are not, after all, very demanding.

Perhaps that is why, unlike me, Edward Lear always hated to admit that his own career was launched by this peculiar five-line lyrical form. Lear actually didn't invent the limerick, even though his name is practically inseparable from it today. Its origins lie shrouded somewhere back in the hoary mists of Irish folklore, fairy tales, and nursery rhymes. In fact, some of the most ancient and familiar lines in English poetry are counted among its number:

> There was an old lady of Leeds
> Who spent all her time in good deeds.
> She worked for the poor
> Till her fingers were sore
> This pious old lady of Leeds.[1]

> Hickory, dickory, dock.
> The mouse ran up the clock.
> The clock struck one,
> The mouse ran down,
> Hickory, dickory, dock.[2]

But, even though the form was already a time-honored convention, it was Lear who first brought the odd pun-filled limerick into popular favor and international fame. He did it quite by accident—and much to his chagrin.

You see, Lear was a mature professional, not a teenage neophyte: His paintings of birds were often compared with Audubon's, his water colors hung in the Louvre, his criticism was widely respected and heeded during his day, and he was often retained to give composition lessons to the sons and daughters of royalty. He apparently was eager to make his mark in history as a serious artist.

Yet he is best remembered for his nonsense verses:

> There was an old man in a tree,
> Who was horribly bored by a bee.
> When they said, "Does it buzz?"
> He replied, "Yes it does!
> It's a regular brute of a bee."[3]

> There was an old man who supposed
> That the street door was partially closed;
> But some very large rats
> Ate his coats and his hats,
> While that futile old gentleman dozed.[4]

Though this kind of nonsense rhyme made him both rich and famous, Lear rather despised them—as a kind of literary junk food. In fact, late in life he said they were "awful and noxious distrac-

tions."[5] Despite his protestations, limericks became one of the
most popular forms of versifying on both sides of the Atlantic during the Victorian age. Their infectious rhythm and lilt appealed to
wits and wags of every stripe.

The more we hear them, the more likely we'll agree with Lear's
stern assessment: Limericks are rather silly. Often only mildly
humorous. Fluff really. Not at all the stuff of serious literature.

Actually, according to Lear, limericks do the opposite of what
"good poetry" is supposed to do. "Like so much else in this poor
fallen world," Lear said, "limericks take the path of least resistance.
They come cheaply and easily. Beware of all such things."[6]

James Q. Wilson, a professor of management and public policy,
makes the same point, not about limericks, but about life. He says:
"The best things in life invariably cost us something. We must sacrifice to attain them, to achieve them, to keep them, even to enjoy
them."[7]

That is one of the most important lessons we can learn in life.
We know we ought to instill that message in our children:
Patience, commitment, diligence, constancy, and discipline will
ultimately pay off if we are willing to defer gratification long
enough for the seeds we have sown to sprout and bear fruit.

A flippant, shallow, and imprecise approach to anything—be it
sports or academics, business or pleasure, friendship or marriage—
is ultimately self-defeating. It is not likely to satisfy any appetite—
at least, not for long. The world is full of seemingly harmless little
distractions; humorous and silly things; banal and trivial things;
things which take the path of least resistance; things which come
cheaply and easily: "Beware of all such things."

We want cheap grace, positive thinking, easy faith. We want Christianity Lite.

Now, that is not to say that we cannot have fun, that we cannot
ever let down our guard, that we are compelled to be continually
intellectually vigilant. On the contrary; some of the most profound
moments in life come when a dad and his kids have tickle fights in

the middle of the living room floor, or when best friends while away the hours together confiding their fondest hopes and dreams, or when brothers and sisters are stricken by a fit of giggles in the grocery store line, or when a grandmom hunkers down to a tiny table for a make-believe afternoon tea party.

But then, moments like these never come cheaply and easily— they are fruit from the carefully tended gardens of love and trust. Lear explains:

> It is all a matter of proportion. There is nothing intrinsically wrong with limericks or any other form of silliness. It is when the shallow things completely supersede and supplant more serious things that we get into trouble. When what people want replaces what people need, then the truth is obscured.[8]

Sadly, that is a lesson nearly lost on us in this odd to-whom-it-may-concern, instant-everything day of microwavable meals, pre-fabricated buildings, bottom-rung bureaucracy, fit-for-the-market education, knee-jerk public misinformation, and predigested formula entertainment. Thus temporary conveniences outweigh permanent virtues.

Even the church has fallen prey to this "spirit of the times." We don't want worship to be too demanding. We don't want doctrine that challenges our pet notions. We want music that we're comfortable with. We want preaching that reassures us, that reinforces our peculiar preferences, that affords us a sense of serenity. We want cheap grace, positive thinking, easy faith. We want Christianity Lite.

It is almost as if we were attempting to reduce the profound truths of the faith to a simple formula—to a kind of theological limerick.

But a genuinely holy and reverent fear of Almighty God cannot be reduced to shallow sentimentalism. Knowing God demands more than soppy feelings or maudlin emotions. Just as the virtues of justice and mercy are not realized in our lives haphazardly, a commitment to spiritual humility requires a walk of determined discipleship. Humble faith is the fruit of a maturity in grace honed over time by unhurried fellowship and everyday obedience.

Sadly, that is not a message proclaimed often in our time. One

only has to look at the modern church's approach to the biblical
disciplines of fasting and prayer to see just how true that is. These
basic building blocks of discipleship were once the hallmarks of
living in humility before God. But apparently, no longer.

Fasting and prayer are not easy. They are not comfortable. They
are unlikely to capture the fascinated attentions of popular fashion
and fancy. So, we don't practice them. Plain and simple. We've relegated them to the long ago and far away.

We'd much rather attend to growth seminars, building programs, demographic surveys, and capital fund-raising campaigns.
Never mind the fact that the Scriptures never once mention
growth seminars, building programs, demographic surveys, and
capital fund-raising campaigns, while fasting and prayer are not
only mentioned, they are mandated.

But then, at a time when the disciplines of the Christian life are
much more like limericks than sonnets—when humble faith is
regarded as little more than a shallow sentiment—this is not all
that surprising.

The Discipline of Fasting

The Hebrew word for *fast* used throughout the Old Testament is
tsome. The Greek word used throughout the New Testament is
nacetis. Both literally mean "to cover over" or "to affix." The idea is
not simply to cover over the mouth—and thus to refrain from eat-
ing—but to affix the attentions to other matters altogether. It is "to
focus on" or "to fasten on" spiritual matters rather than merely temporal matters. It is "to hold fast" to Christ—and nothing else. It is
to abstain from one thing in order to attain to another.

Only by a slow and patient walk in grace are we able to fully
comprehend that "man does not live on bread alone" (Matthew 4:4).
God has appointed fasting to help us realize anew that Christ has
liberated us from the tyranny of the flesh and from the awful surrender of the spirit to the body and its appetite. It is a mighty
reminder for us to humble ourselves "under God's mighty hand"
(1 Peter 5:6).

Whenever and wherever it is mentioned in the Bible, this gracious appointment of the mature Christian life—the discipline of
fasting—has a conspicuous role in humbling God's people so that
they can concentrate on spiritual things:

- Joshua and the elders kept a solemn fast after their people were defeated by the men of Ai (Joshua 7:6).

- When Queen Esther felt herself and her people to be in danger from the conspiracy of Haman, she set apart a season of solemn prayer and fasting (Esther 4:16).

- David fasted and prayed in humiliation in the aftermath of the Bathsheba incident (2 Samuel 12:16).

- The inhabitants of Nineveh set apart a season of special prayer and fasting following Jonah's pronouncement of judgment (Jonah 3:7–8).

- Even the hardened Ahab fasted and cried for mercy when the judgment of God was denounced against him by Elijah (1 Kings 21:27).

- In the New Testament, we see the pious prophetess Anna engaged in serving God day and night with fastings and prayers (Luke 2:37).

- And even our Lord Jesus entered on His public ministry only after a long season of preparatory fasting (Matthew 4:2).

Mentioned more than seventy-five times in the Bible—more than baptism, the Lord's Supper, witnessing, or even tithing—fasting is one of the most basic and essential disciplines of the Christian life.

Living in these limerick-like times, the very idea of fasting seems a bit old-fashioned and ritualistic. Perhaps a tad legalistic. Maybe even bordering on fanatical. But from a biblical perspective it is just a normal aspect of humble faith.

In the Sermon on the Mount, Jesus drives home the importance of normal, regular fasting with a warning, a command, and a promise:

> When you fast, do not look somber as the hypocrites do, for they disfigure their faces to show men they are fasting. I tell you the truth, they have received their reward in full. But when you fast, put oil on your head and wash your face, so that it will not be obvious to men that you are fasting, but only to your Father, who is unseen; and your Father, who sees what is done in secret, will reward you. (Matthew 6:16–18)

First, notice that fasting is not an exercise of ritual correctness for those who want to put on holier-than-thou airs. Jesus says that when we fast, we are not to look like it. None of that baptized-in-vinegar look. No woe-is-me-I'm-in-the-midst-of-a-spiritual-trial expression to wrinkle our nose or mar our visage. Fasting is supposed to evoke humility. If we fast for some outward, physiological, or social benefit; if we fast for whatever sympathy, empathy, or kudos we can muster, then we have already received our reward in full. "Do not disfigure your face as the hypocrites do"—that is the warning.

Second, fasting is to be a part of our regular routine. It is to be woven seamlessly into our normal lifestyles. It is to be fully integrated into our walk with both God and man—with a minimum of disruption. We're to do good—but we're to look good while doing it. "Anoint your head, and wash your face"—that is the command.

Third, fasting is Godward in its orientation. Its only audience is Him. Its only intent is Him. Its only object is Him. It is wholly and completely subsumed in Him. "And your Father, who sees what is done in secret, will repay you"—that is the promise.

Inherent in all three—the warning, the command, and the promise—is the assumption that no matter what, one way or another, the disciples will fast. That much is understood. It is assumed. It is a given. "When you fast," Jesus says twice. No ifs, ands, or buts about it. "When." Our fasting may be absolute (Deuteronomy 9:9) or partial (Daniel 10:3). It may be entirely private (Nehemiah 1:4) or demonstrably corporate (Jeremiah 36:6). It may be occasional (Acts 13:3) or seasonal (Zechariah 8:19). But one thing is certain: If we are followers of Christ; if we are genuine Christian disciples; if we are seriously seeking the will of God, obeying His Word, and walking in dependence on Him, we will fast.

It is interesting to consider that Adam and Eve lost both their spiritual purity and their temporal paradise—all because they failed to fast at the appropriate time.

It is equally interesting to survey the annals of history to discover that virtually all the heroes of the faith through the ages have put a high priority on fasting. From Athanasius to Augustine, from Polycarp to Patrick, from John Chrysostom to John Calvin, from Brother Andrew to Mother Teresa, and from Francis of Assisi to

Francis Schaeffer, the saints through the ages have taken advantage of every appointment of grace—not the least of which was fasting.[9] Not only that, but they encouraged their churches, their communities, and their nations to do likewise. It is common to find references to whole congregations consecrating themselves to covenantal fasts and solemn assemblies. Calls by national leaders for days of prayer and fasting were regular occurrences throughout the West during the glory days of Christendom.[10] Washington, Adams, Jackson, Lee, Davis, Harding, Coolidge, and Eisenhower all stood foursquare in that tradition of "seeking first the kingdom" by establishing regular days of national repentance and fasting.[11]

> ## Regular seasons of prayer are essential to spiritual humility— which is why spiritual humility seems to be so terribly scarce.

It would have been inconceivable to any of them to neglect such an essential aspect of humble discipleship—as inconceivable as substituting recovery for repentance, serenity for sanctification, limericks for the law of God, or choruses for creeds.

Otto Blumhardt, the great seventeenth-century Lutheran missionary, speculated that should the day ever come when such substitutions did actually occur, the minions of the "culture war" would be the least of our worries. He said:

> On the day the church abandons its care of the poor, its fervent ministry of supplication, and its intently chosen fast—for whatever good will or intentions—on that day we will undoubtedly see its clergy dragged off in wickedness and promiscuity, its parishes awhoring after greed and avarice, and its congregations awash in every vain imagination and unspeakable perversion. On that day, the church will cease to be the church. May it never be. May it never be. Stay that day with the hand of faithful diligence, I pray. Stay that day with the fastening of faith.[12]

The Discipline of Prayer

Prayer is the most common Christian expression of humble

faith; but like fasting it may be among the least practiced Christian disciplines. It is said that prayer is the universal language of the soul; but it is actually the solitary province of the supplicating saint. Prayer, as the unconscious heart-cry in times of distress, is the currency of all humanity; but prayer, as the deep and committed soul-bond in communion with Almighty God, is an exceptionally rare and precious jewel.

Certainly, regular seasons of prayer are essential to spiritual humility—which is why spiritual humility seems to be so scarce. We take our time with God in snatches. We throw out petitions rapid-fire on the run. At best, we rush through our laundry lists of wants and needs. Even in the corporate life of the church, prayer gets short shrift—only briefly imposed like talismans at predictable intervals in worship services, business meetings, and meals. And thus we prove the mettle of our woefully insubstantial and unresolved limerick-like faith.

The great romantic poet Samuel Taylor Coleridge observed:

> The act of praying is the very highest energy of which the human mind is capable; praying that is, with the total concentration of the faculties on God. The great mass of worldly men, learned men, and yea, even religious men are absolutely incapable of prayer.[13]

In contrast, the heroes of the faith through the ages have always been diligent, vigilant, and constant in prayer. They humbled themselves before God with prayers, petitions, and supplications, always acknowledging their utter dependence upon His mercy and grace. Athanasius prayed five hours each day.[14] Augustine once set aside eighteen months to do nothing but pray.[15] Bernard of Clairveaux would not begin his daily activities until he had spent at least three hours in prayer.

John Wesley spent two hours daily in prayer—beginning well before dawn.[16] John Fletcher regularly spent all night in prayer. His greeting to friends was always, "Do I meet you praying?"[17]

Martin Luther often commented, "I have so much business I cannot get on without spending three hours daily in prayer."[18] Samuel Rutherford began praying at three.

John Calvin, John Knox, and Theodore Beza vowed to one another to devote two hours daily to prayer. John Welch thought the day ill-spent if he did not spend eight or ten hours in prayer.

"The story of prayer," E. M. Bounds once said, "is the story of great achievements." Indeed, it is. Homer W. Hodge argued:

> Oh, for determined men and women who will rise early and really burn for God. Oh, for a faith that will sweep into heaven with the early dawning of morning and have ships from a shoreless sea loaded in the soul's harbor ere the ordinary laborer has knocked the dew from the scythe or the lackluster has turned from his pallet of straw to spread nature's treasures of fruit before the early buyers. Oh, for such.[19]

Not surprisingly, the Scriptures are brimming over with exhortations to be constant in prayer.

Prayer is to be habitual. It is the expression of our relationship with God.

We are to pray.

We are to pray with wholeheartedness. We are to pray with contrition. We are to pray with all faith. We are to pray with righteous fervor. We are to pray out of obedience and with full confidence. We are to pray in the morning, and in the evening, during the night watch, and at all other times.

God has given us access to His throne and fellowship with Christ. And He expects us to make use of that glorious privilege at every opportunity.

Throughout the Scriptures the priority place of prayer is more than evident in the lives and ministries of God's chosen people:

- Abraham was a man of prayer. He was "the friend of God" and thus enjoyed close and intimate relations with Him (Genesis 15).

- Moses was constant in his fellowship with God. When the nation of Israel rebelled against the Lord and against His appointed leaders, Moses sought mercy and long-suffering on their behalf (Numbers 14:11–38).

- David prayed as he arose in the dawning of the day, yielding the very meditations of his heart to the scrutiny of the Lord (Psalm 5:1–3).

- Solomon prayed before the altar of the Lord in the presence of all the congregation. He interceded on behalf of the nation, for the renewal of the covenant, and for the blessings of providence (1 Kings 8:22–53).

- Elijah prayed during his dramatic confrontation with Ahab, Jezebel, and the prophets of Baal on Mount Carmel (1 Kings 18:36–37).

- Though naked, beaten, imprisoned, and shackled, Paul and Silas were praying and singing hymns to God in the inner prison of Philippi (Acts 16:25).

In the Sermon on the Mount, Jesus not only taught His disciples about fasting, He taught them about prayer:

> And when you pray, do not be like the hypocrites, for they love to pray standing in the synagogues and on the street corners to be seen by men. I tell you the truth, they have received their reward in full. But when you pray, go into your room, close the door and pray to your Father, who is unseen. Then your Father, who sees what is done in secret, will reward you. And when you pray, do not keep on babbling like pagans, for they think they will be heard because of their many words. Do not be like them, for your Father knows what you need before you ask him. (Matthew 6:5–8)

Following these basic introductory instructions, He gave them His model for prayer—known as the Lord's Prayer:

> This, then, is how you should pray: "Our Father in heaven, hallowed be your name, your kingdom come, your will be done on earth as it is in heaven. Give us today our daily bread. Forgive us our debts, as we also have forgiven our debtors. And lead us not into temptation, but deliver us from the evil one." (Matthew 6:9–13)

As He did with fasting, Jesus drives home the importance of consistent, committed prayer with a warning, a command, and a promise.

First, notice that prayer is not a means for self-promotion— either before men or before God. The throne room of the Most

High is not some kind of cosmic vending machine for our every want, whim, or worry any more than it is a showcase for our eloquence or our reverence. It is instead a schoolhouse for humility. Others make a spectacle of themselves when they pray that way. "Do not be like them." That is the warning.

Second, prayer is to be habitual. It is the expression of our relationship with God. It is to be intimate. It is to be personal. It is to be as practical as our daily bread. It is to be as lofty as the outworkings of providence in heaven and on earth. It is to be as pointed as our trespasses and our trespassers. But above all, it is to be regular. "When you pray," Jesus said. "In this manner, therefore, pray." That is the command.

Third, prayer is objectively hedged by God's will. As the *Shorter Catechism of the Westminster Confession* says, "Prayer is an offering up of our desires unto God for things agreeable to His will."[20] We are not to pray simply in order to get something. We are to pray in order to *be* something (James 4:3). We pray in order to be conformed to God's will. And "He who sees in secret will reward openly," for He "knows the things we have need of before we ask Him." That is the promise.

And oh, what a promise!

In accord with the good providence of God, prayer binds and it looses. It casts down and it raises up. It ushers in peace, forgiveness, healing, liberty, wisdom, and protection. Clearly, "the prayer of a righteous man is powerful and effective" (James 5:16).

Samuel Chadwick, a Puritan of great renown, aptly wrote:

> Satan dreads nothing but prayer. Activities are multiplied that prayer may be ousted, and organizations are increased that prayer may have no chance. The one concern of the devil is to keep the saints from praying. He fears nothing from prayerless studies, prayerless work, prayerless religion. He laughs at our toil, mocks at our wisdom, but trembles when we pray.[21]

The Nehemiah Model

Nehemiah was undoubtedly a man of decisive action. He was assuredly a man of vast influence. But in the time of crisis, instead of throwing his political weight around, exercising his political clout, calling in his political favors, and organizing his political resources, Nehemiah fasted and prayed. Instead of charging boldly before the throne of Artaxerxes, he humbled himself before the throne of God, fasted, wept, and prayed:

> I confess the sins we Israelites, including myself and my father's house, have committed against you. We have acted very wickedly toward you. We have not obeyed the commands, decrees and laws you gave your servant Moses. Remember the instruction you gave your servant Moses, saying, "If you are unfaithful, I will scatter you among the nations, but if you return to me and obey my commands, then even if your exiled people are at the farthest horizon, I will gather them from there and bring them to the place I have chosen as a dwelling for my Name." (Nehemiah 1:6–9)

He reminded God that Israel was His people, and he prayed that he would receive mercy at the hand of the king so that his request would be granted.

For an entire month he fasted and prayed (Nehemiah 1:1; 2:1).

His response to the crisis in Jerusalem speaks volumes about his character and about the character of his faith. He understood clearly the consequences of sin. He had a good grasp of the dynamics of history. He showed a thorough understanding of divine providence. He obviously understood the multi-generational nature of the kingdom task. His response gives testimony to his utter dependence upon God and his confidence in biblical problem-solving. He wanted to do things God's way, in God's time, with God's help, in accord with God's will. He lived a life of spiritual humility.

So, he fasted and prayed.

And not just this once. His commitment to these disciplines marked his life throughout his entire career. At every turn, Nehemiah demonstrated devotion to the Lord God on high. When he appeared before Artaxerxes to make petition to rebuild the walls of Jerusalem—fresh from a month of fasting and prayer—he once again breathed a prayer of supplication (Nehemiah 2:4). When threats of violence and conspiracy jeopardized the fledgling reconstruction project, he sought the face of God (4:2–4). When there were conflicts and crises among the people that required his judicious hand, first he prayed (5:19). When an attempt on his life threatened the entire project, he didn't

panic—he made petition to the Lord (6:9). When his own
brethren turned against him, he sought heavenly refuge (6:14).
When he led the people to undertake covenant renewal, he called
them to a new season of fasting and prayer (9:1–38). And when
the work on the walls was complete, again, he consecrated the
time in the holy disciplines (13:31).

Of course, fasting and praying wasn't all that he did. But it was
the foundation of all that he did. Like anyone called by God into
the arena of the culture, he lived out the full dimensions of an integrated biblical worldview. He invested himself in careful planning
(Nehemiah 2:5–6). He laid the groundwork with cautious attention to detail (2:7–8). He enlisted qualified help (2:9). He encouraged his workers (2:17–18). He motivated them (4:14–20). He
organized and delegated the various tasks (3:1–32). He anticipated
difficulty and made provision for it (2:19–20; 6:1–14). He impro-
vised when he had to (4:21–23). He sacrificed (5:14–19), led
(13:4–30), and governed (7:1–7). But undergirding all these necessary activities was his constant reliance upon Almighty God.
Undergirding them all was a humble faith marked by fasting and
prayer.

Nehemiah was confident that God would give him success. He
was sure God would give him strength, show him favor, and see
him through. He was unwavering in his optimism because the work
was conceived by God, not by him. It was God's project, not his.

Nehemiah wanted to be conformed to God's will. He wanted to
be used in God's work. He wanted to be obedient.

And his humble devotional life was a gracious means to that
end.

How Should We Then Live?

Like Nehemiah, we live in a time of crisis. We live in a day of
disintegrating forces—when the very fabric of our civilization is in
jeopardy. When immorality and dishonesty are very nearly behav-
ioral norms while righteousness and sanctification have become
cultural laughingstocks. In such a time, at such a moment, how
should we live?

Instead of responding like Nehemiah did, all too often I am
afraid we are a bit limerick-like:

There were three little birds in a wood
Who always sang hymns when they could.
What the words were about
They could never make out.
But they felt it was doing them good.[22]

Will that kind of limerick-level commitment, limerick-level discipleship, limerick-level faith suffice in these dire days? Hardly.

The Bible tells us that in the past when God's people sought to strengthen their devotional life—to sharpen their intercessions and give passion to their supplications—they fasted and prayed. When they were intent on seeking God's guidance in difficult times, they fasted and prayed (Acts 14:23). When they were wont to express grief—whether over the consequences of their own sins or the sins of others—they fasted and prayed (2 Samuel 1:11–12). When they sought deliverance or protection in times of trouble, they fasted and prayed (2 Chronicles 20:3–4). When they wanted to express repentance and a return to the fold of faith, they fasted and prayed (Joel 2:12). When they wanted to demonstrate humility before the throne of God, they fasted and prayed (Psalm 35:13). When they expressed concern for the ongoing work of the ministry, they fasted and prayed (Daniel 9:3). When they wished to minister to the needs of others, they fasted and prayed (Isaiah 58:6–7). When they sought to overcome temptation and dedicate themselves to holiness, they fasted and prayed (Matthew 4:1–11). When they wanted to express their highest love, honor, worship, and praise to the Father, they fasted and prayed (Luke 2:37). They fasted and prayed as a mark of true discipleship and profound humility.

Long ago, the Byzantine theologian Adeimantos of Thesily wrote: "Upon these hang the whole of our outward expression of faith, of hope, and of love: prayer and fasting."[23]

For many—whose god seems to be their stomach—this is a radical notion. But from the biblical perspective, there is hardly a better way to "taste and see that the Lord is good." There is hardly a more effective means of appropriating God's grace—thus "fastening faith" to surer foundations than mere appetites and desires can allow.

Not that we really have a choice about the matter; this is the normal maturation of the Christian life in spiritual humility and divine grace.

Thus, while he still occupied the White House, Calvin Coolidge wrote:

> There are those who suppose that when it comes to matters of religion, we all have the prerogative to pick and choose what we will and will not believe or observe. But according to the Christian religion, it is God who does the picking and choosing. Our job is simply to submit. Of course, that's the problem, isn't it? It is never simple to simply submit.[24]

Right Where He Wants Us

I don't know about you, but I'm not good enough to live out the full implications of the Micah Mandate. I'm not disciplined enough. I get hungry and distracted. It is easier for me to live life on the level of limericks. I'm just not a sonnet sort of guy. I'm not personally qualified for holiness. But then, I'm not really qualified for any of the important roles I find myself filling in this life either—such as that of a father or a husband.

I remember only too well the sense of blinding panic I felt the first time I held my firstborn in my arms. I just kept thinking over and over again: "What on earth have I gotten myself into?"

As I gazed down in wonder at his red little face, with tears streaming down my cheeks, I was forced to realize that I was no less helpless than he.

Which is right were God wanted me. And still does. And you no less than me. Dependent upon His grace—utterly, completely, and entirely—both to do what God wants us to do and to be what God wants us to be. That is humility.

According to Oswald Chambers: "We cannot save ourselves nor sanctify ourselves, God does that; but God will not give us good habits, He will not give us character, He will not make us walk aright."

The prophet Micah told the people of his day that God did not want their sacrifices, their gifts, or their very bodies (Micah 6:7). Instead, He desired another "good" altogether (Micah 6:8). He wanted them to "look to God" for their all-in-all (Micah 7:7). He "required" them (Micah 6:8).

Our walk of holiness and humility—evidenced in our adherence to the devotional disciplines of the faith—is a sure sign that we have indeed offered ourselves up as "living sacrifices, holy and pleasing to God" (Romans 12:1). And that is the essence of the Micah Mandate.

HUMBLING EXPERIENCES
"He has showed you, O man, what is good. And what does the Lord require of you? To act justly and to love mercy and to walk humbly with your God"
(Micah 6:8).

Humble discipline has always been among the most highly appreciated characteristics of the heroes of the faith. Across the span of history those who have made the greatest impact for the greatest good have invariably been those who have walked in quiet obedience and holy fear of God. Examples abound:

Athanasius (300–373) was one of the giants of the church's Patristic Age. As a young deacon from Alexandria, he attended the First Ecumenical Council at Nicaea, where he took a leading role in shaping the Nicene Creed. His bold defense of the doctrine of the trinity against the Arian heresy demanded his attentions throughout his life and resulted in repeated exiles from his beloved home. He was also involved in various conflicts in the arena of politics, the arts, liturgical renewal, monastic development, New Testament canonicity, and judicial reform. He wrote several important works including biographies, commentaries, systematic theologies, and devotional treatises. His short classic, *On the Incarnation*, is still a staple of any solid theological education. Yet despite a life filled with furious activity and controversy, it was for his personal piety and humble faith that he earned for himself the sobriquet "Athanasius *conta mundum*," or "Athanasius against the world." Long seasons of prayer and fasting punctuated his life with an air of humility and faithfulness that his opponents simply were unable to match.

Henry Meldith (1544–72) was a young Huguenot pastor in

central Navarre renowned for his holiness and humility. During the early days of the Reformation—when passions were high and tempers were short—he taught his congregation discretion and long-suffering through an exercise of the basic biblical disciplines of prayer and fasting. In a society riven by political and theological strife, they were able to build bridges of reconciliation. Meldith himself became a legate to Henry of Navarre, who eventually assumed the throne of France. He carried a message of humility, faithfulness, and quiet obedience to the great conferences of Poissy in 1561 and New Rochelle in 1571. Several accounts of those meetings note the powerful influence his prayerful attitude and life of discipline had upon the other attendees. That he was accidentally killed in the riotous St. Bartholomew Day Massacre in Paris the following year probably sealed the fate of the Huguenot community more than any other single event. The still wavering king lamented his death as "the loss of France's humblest Christian."[25]

In 1625, *Nicholas Ferrar* (1579–1637) retired from a promising parliamentary career in London and moved to a Christian community in Huntingdonshire. The community was marked by extreme Puritan piety: They fasted regularly—both publicly and privately; twice a day they all attended the liturgical offices in their tiny church; at every hour during the day some members joined in a little office of prayer so that the whole psalter was recited daily; and at night, at least two members of the household maintained a "nightwatch of prayer" and the psalter was again recited. They were marked by their charity and pro-life activism as well—so that their spiritual disciplines were not merely turned inward. Ferrar focused their practical and merciful concerns on abandoned boys who roamed the byways. Ultimately, the community developed one of the most effective alternatives to the humanism of the day through simple Christian service and unfaltering spiritual devotion.

Dozens of others could be cited throughout the wide span of history: Benedict of Nursia (d. 550), Gerald of Mayo (d. 732), Martin Bucer (d. 1551), Thomas

Cranmer (d. 1556), Gemma Galgani (d. 1903), Lottie Moon (d. 1912), and E. M. Bounds (d. 1913). Each demonstrated a humbleness of life and faith through careful attention to the basic Christian disciplines: prayer and fasting. And as a result, they left their mark upon eternity as well as upon history.

THE DISCIPLINE OF HUMILITY

*"He has showed you, O man, what is good.
And what does the Lord require of you? To act
justly and to love mercy and to walk humbly
with your God" (Micah 6:8).*

Read the startlingly contemporary prophetic message of Isaiah 58. Notice how internal disciplines are directly correlated to external societal conditions. How does this correlation reinforce the message of Isaiah's colleague, Micah? What implications does it have for the church in our day?

Biographies of Christian heroes offer revealing glimpses into the devotional lives and habits of those who have gone before us in faith. Make it a point, whenever you read about believers in the past, to take note of the central place of prayer and fasting in their everyday affairs. We really ought to pass on such stirring stories of faithfulness, diligence, and obedience in days gone by—so try to weave them into your conversations and tell them to your children. Often the first step toward imitation is inspiration.

Books on prayer and the various other disciplines of holiness abound. And certainly, it is a good thing to read them. But it is an even better thing to put them into practice. Make a commitment to get past Square One. You don't really need all the latest discipleship gizmos and gadgets, just resolve to walk in faith: Just do it.

Discipline is hardest when attempted alone. We all need accountability. Why not ask a friend to help reinforce your conviction to avoid limerick-like superficiality and to get serious about prayer and fasting? Or maybe you can start a small accountability group at your church so several people can bolster and strengthen one another.

Though all too often encrusted by unthinking ritual and unexamined habit, the liturgical church calendar was originally designed to be an aid to our devotional lives—to give order and structure to our times of prayer and fasting. Why not revisit the calendar with an eye toward reigniting your comprehension of God's redemptive plan for and through the ages?

Notes

1. Karen Gascony, *An Anthology of Limericks* (London: Frontline, 1990), 34.

2. Ibid., 71.

3. Louis Untermeyer, ed., *Lots of Limericks* (New York: Bell, 1961), 27.

4. Ibid., 23.

5. Russell Thom Nye, *Edward Lear* (Brighton, U.K.: Alfaeric Mews, 1988), 88.

6. Ibid., 89.

7. *The Spectator*, 5 March 1994.

8. Nye, 90.

9. Basil Konaric, *Synaxarion: Fasting and Liturgy* (Toronto: Orthodox Troparion, 1981), 128; Steven Huntington, *Puritan Discipline* (Tulsa, Okla.: Reformed Baptist, 1973), xi; Gordont Darby, *Fasting* (Hargrave, U.K.: Lightway, 1987), 3; and Arthur Wallis, *God's Chosen Fast* (Eastbourne, U.K.: Victory, 1969).

10. Darby, 5–9.

11. Ibid.

12. Maria L. H. Blumhardt, *Pioneer to Africa* (St. Louis, Mo.: Wittenburg, 1949), 6.

13. Ken Leighton, *The High Call of Prayer* (Kensington, U.K.: Victory, 1970), 56.

14. Konaric, 129.

15. Ibid.

16. Ibid.

17. Ibid., 37.

18. Ibid.

19. Homer W. Hodge, *Anthology* (Atlanta: Gospel Press, 1927), 34–35.

20. *The Confession of Faith* (Richmond, Va.: John Knox, 1944).

21. David Bullock, *Puritan Piety* (Edinburgh, U.K.: Kirk House, 1956), 103.

22. Gascony, 64.

23. Konaric, 131.

24. Elmer Jansen, *Faith in the White House* (New York: Harlen, 1966), 34.

25. Gerard Hellenique, *The Huguenots* (New York: Ypres Press, 1975), 177.

PART FIVE

THE RIGHT BALANCE

*As pride sometimes is hid under humility, idleness
is often covered by turbulence and hurry.*
Samuel Johnson

HAVING IT ALL

*Those who have no concern for their ancestors
will, by simple application of the same
rule, have none for their descendants.*
Richard Weaver

V ienna is the beautiful and historic hub of Central and Eastern Europe—just as it has been for more than one thousand years. Thus, it is an international city unlike any other. London, New York, and Paris all boast diverse and multi-cultural communities—the legacy of far-flung empires and financial interests. But Vienna's character is drawn from a kind of supra-nationalism unique to Hapsburg domains. Here Northern Europe meets the Balkans, Western Europe meets the Steppes, and the Alps tumble down toward the Adriatic. Vienna serves as a vast roiling mix of peoples and traditions. But instead of being a melting pot, it is more like a cauldron of its famed goulash—deliciously incongruous.

The airport, roads, and hotels are all high-tech German, but the food, hospitality, and music are all old-world Hapsburg. It is a seductive place with magnificent theaters, resplendent palaces, and broad, bustling boulevards. But all the strains of Vienna's wide-ranging heritage are most evident at the Stephansdomplatz—the city's beautiful Gothic cathedral.

Consecrated as a Romanesque basilica in 1147, the church has endured the tumult of war, fire, plague, revolution, conquest, and imperial ambition. Over the years, vast Gothic towers, chapels, vaults, spires, and portals were added in a wild variety of architectural textures and scales. Yet in the end, they all seem to harmonize with one another beautifully.

Whenever I am able to visit the great church, I am reminded of the nature of the body of Christ—the eternal church, not made of bricks and mortar. The topsy-turvy adventure that the Gospel inevitably spawns among believers is as oddly paradoxical as that ancient structure—but not just because it is improbably diverse yet unified. It is because the whole feat of beauty and balance was achieved by God through anonymous, ordinary people.

Certainly the imperial House of Hapsburg employed a few master craftsmen from time to time over the years to complete one project or another in the cathedral. But the vast majority of the construction was undertaken by the faithful members of the congregation. There were virtually no professional artisans. There were practically no renowned architects. There were no corporate contractors, no certified engineers, and no planning commissions. That feat of stupendous architectural beauty was accomplished by the simple men and women at hand. The extraordinary was achieved by the ordinary.

That is actually the great lesson of all of history. It has always been ordinary people who ultimately were the ones to shape the outcome of great human events—not kings and princes, not masters and tyrants. It has always been laborers and workmen, cousins and acquaintances who have upended the expectations of the brilliant and the glamorous, the expert and the meticulous. It has been plain folks, simple people, who have changed the course of history—because they are the stuff of which history is made.

Most of the grand-glorious headline-making events through the ages have been little more than backdrops to the real drama of grocers, village cobblers, next-door neighbors, and grandfathers. Despite all the hype, hoopla, and hysteria of sensational turns-of-events, the ordinary people who tend their gardens and rear their children and perfect their trades and mind their businesses are the ones who make or break a culture. Just as they always have. Just as they always will.

Whether building cathedrals like the Stephansdomplatz, toppling empires like the Soviet Union, or establishing justice, mercy, and humble faith in this poor fallen world, all of history's most significant developments have been wrought by shopkeepers and students, dads and daughters, peasants and populists.

Intellectuals and elitists hesitate to admit it, but the accomplishments of the quiet and the unsung actually outstrip the loudly publicized deeds of the rich and the regarded. Those who write the histories and steer the cultural apparatus are wont to regard the gifts of ordinary people with scorn, but they are in the end overwhelmed by the torrent of truth evident in God's good providence in the course of time.

That is precisely why the Christian worldview stands out so brilliantly against the dullness of modern thought—it is brilliant because it is mundane. The Christian faith has always acknowledged that a community's strength is not in its leaders; it is in its average citizens. It recognizes that the real decision-makers in any culture are the anonymous plodders. These secret heroes show consistent attention to the details that actually matter—enjoying their wives, loving their children, helping their neighbors, worshiping in Spirit and in truth, seeking righteousness, and applying their unique gifts to the affairs of everyday life. Thus, the masters of the universe are not muscle-bound Greek gods come down from Olympus. They are ordinary folks—believers like you and me.

> Every member of the body of
> Christ, however humble, however
> obscure, however feeble, and
> however despised by the people
> of this world, is vital to the
> overall work of the ministry.

The Micah Mandate appears at first glance to be a part of the repertoire of the especially skilled, the prepared, and the qualified. It looks and sounds hard—like an unscalable summit of spiritual heights. It appears to be attainable only for the select few, the elite, and the privileged. Like some kind of spiritual juggling act or devotional gymnastics, it seems to be an ideal for the fit, the ambitious, and the talented.

But nothing could be further from the truth. Like the building of cathedrals, the Micah Mandate is peculiarly the domain of the ordinary. The simplest people doing the simplest things has always been the most profound course to achieve the most profound things.

When we understand that, we will be able to actually do it.

Priestly Service

"Church architecture," according to the great medieval builder and designer Michel di Giovanni, "ought to be an earthly and temporal fulfillment of the Savior's own prophesy that though the voices of men be still, the rocks and stones themselves will cry out with the laud and praise and honor due unto the King of kings and the Lord of lords."[1]

We don't have to fabricate cathedral bells, towers, and spires to transform the most mundane things into the most glorious, though. The fact is, God has dispersed among His people a rich treasury of spiritual gifts that equip and enable even the plainest of us to contribute magnificently to the work of the Gospel in the world. Every member of the body of Christ, however humble, however obscure, however feeble, and however despised by the people of this world, is vital to the overall work of the ministry.

This notion, often called the doctrine of the priesthood of believers, was the cornerstone of the Reformation. It was at the crux of the struggle over justification, ecclesiastical authority, and even mysticism in worship that pitted Martin Luther against Erasmus, Eck, and ultimately the pope himself. Later, it was at issue when John Calvin came into conflict with the city council of Geneva and when John Knox confronted Mary Queen of Scots. According to historian Philip Schaff, "The doctrine of the priesthood of believers was at the very heart of the principle of Protestantism."[2]

But the doctrine was no sixteenth-century innovation. In fact, the notion that all believers are responsible to "prepare God's people for works of service" (Ephesians 4:12) and to exercise their gifts (Romans 12:6) is as ancient as revelation itself. Even the earliest stories of God's redemptive work make this plain.

For example, the tragic record of Sodom and Gomorrah can be

understood best through the lens of this important doctrine. The
two cities were obviously consumed with vile and detestable sin
early on in their recorded history. The people there were perverse
(Genesis 19:5). They were violent (Genesis 19:9). They were arro-
gant, careless, and selfish (Ezekiel 16:49). They were haughty, self-
destructive, and abominable (Ezekiel 16:50). They were utterly
wicked (Genesis 18:20).

But that is not why God ultimately judged and destroyed them.
Despite all the debauchery, lasciviousness, and blasphemy, the
Bible makes clear that God was more than willing to spare the
cities—even after He had pronounced His intended judgment:

> Abraham approached [the Lord] and said: "Will You sweep away
> the righteous with the wicked? What if there are fifty righteous
> people in the city? Will you really sweep it away and not spare the
> place for the sake of the fifty righteous people in it? Far be it from
> you to do such a thing—to kill the righteous with the wicked,
> treating the righteous and the wicked alike. Far be it from you!
> Will not the Judge of all the earth do right?" The Lord said, "If I
> find fifty righteous people in the city of Sodom, I will spare the
> whole place for their sake." (Genesis 18:23–26)

Abraham appealed to the Lord just before the intended destruction of Sodom and Gomorrah. God responded that if fifty men
could be found who were, in effect, guarding the city with their
righteousness, then He would relent.

So, Abraham decides to bargain some more:

> Then Abraham spoke up again: "Now that I have been so bold as
> to speak to the Lord, though I am nothing but dust and ashes,
> what if the number of the righteous is five less than fifty? Will you
> destroy the whole city because of five people?" "If I find forty-five
> there," he said, "I will not destroy it." (Genesis 18:27–28)

Again, God told Abraham, He would spare the cities if only
there were forty-five good men guarding the people with their
righteousness.

> Once again he spoke to him, "What if only forty are found there?"
> He said, "For the sake of forty I will not do it." (Genesis 18:29)

God would spare the city and acknowledge the preserving
power of just forty righteous men.

> Then he said, "May the Lord not be angry, but let me speak. What
> if only thirty can be found there?" He answered, "I will not do it if
> I find thirty there." (Genesis 18:30)

Even "a little yeast works through the whole batch of dough"
(1 Corinthians 5:6). God told Abraham that He would not judge
the city on account of the protection afforded by just thirty righteous men.

> And he said, "Now that I have been so bold as to speak to the
> Lord, what if only twenty can be found there?" He said, "For the
> sake of twenty, I will not destroy it." (Genesis 18:31)

Even twenty guardians were enough to stay the hand of execu-
tion.

> Then he said, "May the Lord not be angry, but let me speak just
> once more. What if only ten can be found there?" He answered,
> "For the sake of ten, I will not destroy it." When the Lord had fin-
> ished speaking with Abraham, he left, and Abraham returned
> home. (Genesis 18:32–33)

The moral of this seemingly tedious lesson is abundantly clear:
God will spare the wicked for the sake of the righteous. If good
men will guard the cities, they are safe. But, if there are no such
guardians, disaster is inevitable.

God has always called His people to be priests. The Israelites
were chosen out of all the peoples of the earth to be "a kingdom of
priests" (Exodus 19:6). And since the Day of Pentecost, God has
called the church to be a "holy priesthood" as well (1 Peter 2:5).
The Hebrew word often used for priest in the Old Testament is
kohen. It literally means "to serve," "to minister," or "to guard." The
Greek word often used in the New Testament is *hierateuo*. It also literally means "to serve as a guardian" or "to minister." Thus a priest
is someone who protects. He preserves. He ministers mercy and
stays the hand of destruction and defilement. He serves those
around him as a kind of spiritual watchman or guard.

Throughout the Bible those who were called to the priestly
office were given the responsibility to mercifully protect the people through holy service:

• Adam was called to serve as a priest. He was to cultivate and guard the garden (Genesis 2:15). But he failed to do his duty and the calamity of the Fall resulted (Genesis 3:1–19).

- Aaron was called to serve as a priest. He was to guard the people from sin and shame (Exodus 32:25). But he failed to do his duty, and the people began to worship and revel before a golden calf (Exodus 32:1–6).

- The Levites were called to serve as priests. Why? Because they guarded the integrity of God when all the rest of Israel was consumed with idolatry (Exodus 32:26–29). It was not until the Levites failed to the uttermost that God brought condemnation and judgment upon Israel (Jeremiah 6:13–15).

Mankind was created to be a priest before God. He was made to guard against evil. He was chosen to serve. Thus, the inclination to priesthood is inescapable. Even if he ultimately fails—as Adam, Aaron, and the Levites did—man's impulse to some kind of service remains. If man fails to be a true priest guarding the true sanctuary, he will become a false priest, guarding a false sanctuary. He will turn from selfless service to self-aggrandizing service:

- After the flood, Nimrod, grandson of the accursed Ham, founded the false kingdom of Babel (Genesis 10:8–10). His people, bent on rebellion, "named" themselves priests (Genesis 11:4), and built false sanctuary (Genesis 11:1–4).

- When Jeroboam split Israel in two, taking the ten northern tribes with him, it was inevitable that he too would establish a false kingdom (1 Kings 12:20) and a false sanctuary (1 Kings 12:25–29), served by false priests (1 Kings 12:30–31).

Of course, each of these forays into self-serving priesthood ended in the judgment of God. Only a true priesthood serving in a true sanctuary can offer true protection. When man fails to do his duty, destruction occurs.

Thus, the whole reason Sodom and Gomorrah were destroyed was that the men in the city refused to guard it with their righteousness. They refused to serve as true priests.

In each case where men failed to do their jobs as priest, they lost everything they had. They refused to serve; they refused to live lives of merciful selflessness; they succumbed to sins of omission.

Christians As Priests

It is not surprising to discover that Jesus commissioned His disciples to act as priests, serving and nurturing the nations (Matthew 28:18–20; Acts 1:8). They were to be the caretakers of the waters of life (Revelation 22:17), the bread of life (John 6:31; 1 Corinthians 11:24), and the Word of life (1 John 1:1). They were to preserve and guard the earth. He said to them: "You are the salt of the earth. But if the salt loses its saltiness, how can it be made salty again? It is no longer good for anything, except to be thrown out and trampled by men" (Matthew 5:13).

In the ancient world, salt was highly valued for a number of reasons. It was used to season the food of man and of beast. It was used as a medicine and as a preservative. It was symbolic of loyalty (Numbers 18:19), discretion (Colossians 4:6), purity (Mark 9:49), and perpetuity (2 Chronicles 13:5).

> If the people of God fail to be salt, then even the most providentially privileged nation cannot be preserved from putrefaction; it will fall into judgment.

Interestingly, salt was also the mandatory accompaniment of some of the priestly sacrifices in the Old Testamental period, including the grain (Leviticus 2:13) and burnt offerings (Ezekiel 43:24).

When Jesus told His disciples that they were to be "the salt of the earth" (Matthew 5:13), the immediate priestly implications would have been obvious to them. They were to serve by guarding the nations with their covenantal loyalty in discretion, purity, and perpetuity. They were to be the medicine of hope; they were to be a merciful preserving agent, restraining sin; they were to be living sacrifices.

The survival of any nation depends on the fulfillment of the priestly servanthood duties. If the people of God fail to be salt, then even the most providentially privileged nation cannot be preserved from putrefaction; it will fall into judgment.

Notice that when God describes the priestly task of His people
throughout the Bible, He invariably uses civil or cultural terminol
ogy: We are to be ambassadors (2 Corinthians 5:20), judges
(1 Corinthians 6:3), rulers (Ephesians 1:11), and witnesses (Acts
1:8). Notice too that this language is not simply symbolic.
Whenever God engages His people in the work of guarding a
culture or a land, He establishes them in ministries marked by a
passion for justice, concern for mercy, and a heart of humble
faithfulness.

But this call to be priests guarding the land goes out to every
believer, regardless of background, preparation, or status. Every
Christian is uniquely equipped by the power of the Holy Spirit to
serve those whom God has placed around us.

The doctrine of the priesthood of believers is not selective; it is
universal.

The Micah Mandate's triad of virtues—justice, mercy, and humble faith—is particularly relevant to our call to serve as priests.
Justice is the pursuit of righteous standards in our communities and
our relationships. Eschewing the extremes of left or right, of liberal
or conservative, of Herodian or Pharasaical, it holds up the
Scriptures as the plumb-line and bottom-line for every human
endeavor. Mercy is the personal touch of the Gospel. Where justice
is active, mercy is personal and compassionate. Where justice is no
respecter of persons, mercy extends its respect to all men everywhere. Humble faith is simply the recognition of who God is and
what He has done. It is the awestruck and fearful response of the
redeemed in the face of grace. A true priest cannot possibly carry
out his or her servant responsibilities as salt, light, and guard without a careful practice of each of these virtues. In a very real sense,
the Micah Mandate is a call to fulfill this priesthood role. It challenges each of us to move beyond the immobilized spectator
church of our day into the fullness of the biblical vision of true spirituality and effective ministry. It brings a word of faith, hope, and
love to a needy world on the very brink of disaster. It is the common man's manifesto.

Practical Priesthood

Birmingham, Alabama, was a wild and untamed mining town in

the heart of the reconstructed South when James Alexander Bryan came to pastor the Third Presbyterian Church there in 1888. When he died in 1941, Birmingham had become a vibrant industrial center.

In the years between, Brother Bryan—as he was affectionately called—won the hearts of generation after generation of her citizens.

He was an unlikely hero for the bustling town. For one thing, he was noticeably inadept as a pulpiteer. His sermons were often halting, rambling, and inarticulate. Though entirely committed to the authority of the Scriptures and the centrality of preaching, he simply was not a skilled orator.

He was also a poor administrator. He was notoriously disorganized. When it came to the niggling details of management, he was often absentminded and forgetful. He never seemed to lose sight of the "big picture," but all the necessary increments got lost in the shuffle. Though perpetually busy, he was easily distracted and rarely kept up with his workload.

He didn't even maintain a particularly winsome appearance. He was more often than not disheveled, shabbily dressed, and hastily groomed. He was shy, soft-spoken, and had a slight stutter. In a day and time when manliness and imposing presence were especially esteemed, he was slight and retiring.

Not surprisingly, during his long tenure as pastor, his church never really grew. When he died, membership stood at just under a hundred—right where it was shortly after he arrived in Birmingham a half-century earlier.

Nevertheless, he was practically a cultural icon in the city. Near the end of his life of service, he was honored by local leaders and dignitaries in a citywide celebration. The president of the City Commission said: "No man in Birmingham is better known or better loved than Brother Bryan. There is one man in this city about whom we are all agreed, and he is Brother Bryan."[3]

The editor of the city newspaper agreed: "Brother Bryan is the only man, whom we have ever known, whose motives have never been questioned. He is the one man for whom we are all unanimous."[4]

The city erected a statue of the humble pastor at one of its busiest intersections near downtown. It portrayed him in a posture

of prayer and proclaimed him "the patron saint of Birmingham."[5]
On the occasion of its unveiling, Hugo Black, the Supreme Court
Justice, asserted:

> This dedication raises our community to its loftiest heights, just as
> Brother Bryan has all these long years of his faithful and selfless
> service. The statue, let us hope, will inspire those here today, those
> who know Brother Bryan, and all those who come after, to love
> our neighbors as ourselves, even as he has.[6]

When Brother Bryan died, the entire city mourned his passing.
Thousands of men, women, and children crowded around the tiny
sanctuary and followed the solemn cortege at his funeral. Flags
were lowered to half-mast and the mayor proclaimed an official
day of prayer and fasting. How had this seemingly inept pastor
won over an entire city so completely? How had this painfully
ordinary man accomplished a feat so extraordinary as this?

Very simply, Brother Bryan was a common man who proved to
be an uncommon example of the Micah Mandate. Though he violated all the rules of success, church growth, worldly acclaim, and
effectiveness, he seemed to incarnate the essence of the faith once
and for all delivered unto the saints. He was, as many called him,
"religion in shoes."[7]

He made a circuit every morning just before dawn to all the fac-
tories, shops, fire and police stations, schools, and offices downtown to pray with as many working men and women as he could.
He would simply announce himself, drop to his knees wherever he
was, and begin to intercede for each of them. Over time, his piety
became a cherished emblem of personal concern in a harshly
impersonal industrial world. He was the unofficial chaplain to the
entire community—it was often said that the words most often on
his lips were, "Let us pray."

Brother Bryan also distinguished himself with his selfless service
to the poor, the needy, the brokenhearted, and the sick. His efforts
to encourage the distressed led him to establish several city outreaches to the homeless, to orphans and widows, and to the victims of war and pestilence overseas. More than any rich philan-
thropist, more than any well-endowed foundation, more than any
charitable institution, he demonstrated the power and effect of
merciful service on the fabric of a community.

He was a faithful pro-life stalwart as well. When a Planned Parenthood representative came to Birmingham in 1937, he was a vocal critic—calling on Christians to uphold their legacy of concern and care and thus make the vast organization's services unnecessary and unwanted. Though a confirmed non-partisan politically, he often lobbied magistrates when issues of justice arose—he was, for instance, an early champion of civil rights and racial reconciliation. His character, pure motives, and holy demeanor enabled him to take such controversial stands without polarizing or alienating his beloved fellow citizens. Somehow they understood that his commitment to justice was a natural outgrowth of his humble faith and merciful service—one could not be had without the others.

Like so many heroes of the faith who had gone before him, Brother Bryan put into practice the Reformation doctrine of the priesthood of all believers—he thoroughly integrated the virtues of justice, mercy, and humility before God, conscientiously guarding the land with his righteousness. Like the cathedral builders of ages gone by, he was an ordinary man who nevertheless accomplished extraordinary feats.

On the day following his funeral, the newspaper in Birmingham commented:

> We have had set before us the clearest example of what it must mean to be a follower of Christ. There can be little doubt to anyone familiar with Brother Bryan's life and work that the high ideals of the faith may actually be manifested. And that poses a tremendously prophetic challenge to us all.[8]

Indeed, it does.

GUARDING BALANCE

"He has showed you, O man, what is good. And what does the Lord require of you? To act justly and to love mercy and to walk humbly with your God"
(Micah 6:8).

An integrated balance of justice, mercy, and humble faith has always been a hallmark of the church's heroes.

Never yielding to the easy temptations of one extreme or another, they were ordinary men and women who simply served those around them as priests and servants—thus, guarding the land with their righteousness. Examples abound:

Late in the third century, *Afra of Augsburg* (277–304) developed a ministry to the abandoned children of prisoners, thieves, smugglers, pirates, runaway slaves, and brigands. Herself a former prostitute, she cared for the despised and the rejected with a special fervor, taking them into her home, creating an adoption network, and sacrificing all she had that out of her lack they might be satisfied. Her faith and piety were renowned. Her struggle for justice was unparalleled. And her ministry of mercy was an inspiration to thousands. Ultimately, her well-integrated balanced approach to the work of the Gospel in the world came under the scrutiny of the authorities. Considered a grave danger to state security due to her influence, she was martyred during the great persecution of Diocletian.

John of Amathus (551–620) was born in Cyprus, though he is best known for his work in Egypt. The greater part of his life was spent engaged in public service and civil affairs. He married young and faithfully raised his children in the nurture and admonition of the Lord. Despite the fact that he was entirely untrained in theology, his unflagging personal piety and evident wisdom encouraged the people of Alexandria to call him to be their patriarch and pastor at the age of fifty. He threw himself into his new responsibilities with characteristic zeal. He injected new life into that old church by establishing innumerable ministries to the needy. He endowed several health-care institutions—including the very first maternity hospital. He founded several homes for the aged and infirm. He opened hospices and lodges for travelers. He tore down the remnants of the old infanticide walls outside the city with his own hands and called on his parishioners to join him in defending the sanctity of human life in the future. So prolific were his deeds of justice and mercy that he eventually became known as John the Almsgiver.

John Buchan (1875–1940) was a popular Scottish author and statesman who served the British crown as a diplomat, agent, and colonial governor around the globe—in India, South Africa, Continental Europe, and Canada. He wrote more than sixty books, including several well-regarded biographies, novels, and inspirational commentaries. Though he is best remembered today for his spy thrillers—he practically invented that genre during the calamitous days of the First World War—he was known in his own day as a man of extraordinary balance. He obviously served his nation selflessly through many dangers, toils, and snares. He often worked on behalf of the poor and needy through the innumerable mission projects and programs he sponsored. And he was a pious man who faithfully served as an elder in his local church and as moderator for the Presbyterian General Assembly of the Church of Scotland several years running. He seemed to have it all—and thus lived out the Micah Mandate on a daily basis.

Dozens of others could be cited throughout the wide span of history: Thecla of Iconium (d. 70), Tartian of Lorrai (d. 189), Adamnan of Iona (d. 697), Blaise Pascal (d. 1662), William Wilberforce (d. 1833), B. B. Warfield (d. 1921), Maximilian Kolbe (d. 1941). Each demonstrated a balance in life and faith through a careful integration of justice, mercy, and humility before God. And as a result, they became model "priests" for all who have come after.

THE CHANGING OF THE GUARD

"He has showed you, O man, what is good.
And what does the Lord require of you? To act
justly and to love mercy and to walk humbly
with your God" (Micah 6:8).

Can just one person really make a difference? We know that in the political realm, the involvement of every person does indeed count: In 1645, Oliver Cromwell gained control of England by one vote; in 1776, one vote determined that English, not German, would be the official American language; in 1845, one vote brought Texas into the Union; in 1860, one vote determined that the radical Unitarians would gain control of the Republican Party, thus sparking the War between the States; in 1923, one vote gave Adolf Hitler control of the Nazi Party; in 1960, John F. Kennedy defeated Richard Nixon for the presidency by less than one vote per precinct. Again and again this theme resounds. Survey the Scriptures to underscore this theme in your own mind—focus particularly on the books of Judges and Acts.

Now, examine your own life experience: How many times has an individual, acting faithfully, dramatically influenced you for good? Make a list of those instances of God's good providence through the priestly ministry of others.

What are your gifts? What are you called to do? How should the principles and precepts of the priesthood of believers be manifested in your own life and work? Why not keep a ministry journal documenting the opportunities and challenges God poses for you each day in these arenas?

Notes

1. Harvey Colpepper, *Light Unto the Darkness* (London: Bilthieus Publications, 1981), 22.

2. Arnold Duffy, *The Reformation* (London: Longworth Press, 1977), 97.

3. Hunter Blakely, *Religion in Shoes* (Birmingham, Ala.: Southern University Press, 1989), 146.

4. Ibid.

5. Ibid., 190.

6. Ibid., 191.

7. Ibid., 198.

8. Ibid., 88.

WHERE THE ACTION IS

Since the time of Bacon the world has been
running away from, rather than toward,
first principles, so that, on the verbal level,
we see "fact" substituted for "truth."
Richard Weaver

A s I travel around the country and speak to different groups, I am often asked what I think is the greatest threat to the integrity and security of American life and culture. I suppose that those who ask the question expect me to name one of the many humanistic juggernauts that seem to be forever laying siege to justice, mercy, and humble faith.

Perhaps they expect me to name the American Civil Liberties Union. And for good reason. There can be little doubt that the ACLU has subverted justice in this land to an extraordinary degree.[1] With more than six thousand cases in the courts each year and with a blatantly political agenda, the vast reach of the organization has tragically affected virtually every community and every family in America. But I don't think that it actually poses the gravest threat to our culture today.

Perhaps they expect me to name Planned Parenthood. And for good reason. There can be little doubt that the organization has subverted mercy in this land to an extraordinary degree.[2] With nearly two hundred affiliates and more than eight hundred clinics nationwide, the multi-billion-dollar abortion and sex education conglomerate has defiled the minds of children, exploited the predicaments of the needy, and appropriated the resources of taxpayers in horrifyingly unprecedented ways. But I don't think that it actually poses the gravest threat to our culture today.

Perhaps they expect me to name the National Education Association. Again, for good reason. There can be little doubt that the NEA has subverted humble faith in this land to an extraordinary degree.[3] Now controlling more than 90 percent of the government schools in America, the organization and its army of lobbyists, bureaucrats, and activists are largely responsible for the profound failure of public education today—its ideological extremism, its lack of academic achievement, its brutal administrative centralization, and its insensitivity to the unique integrity of families, schools, or communities. But I don't think that it actually poses the gravest threat to our culture today.

Perhaps they expect me to name some homosexual activist group like Act-Up, an environmentalist group like Greenpeace, a globalist group like the United Nations, or a New Age group like Tikkun. And certainly each of these organizations ought to raise our alarms and cause us great concern. But I don't think that any of them actually poses the gravest threat to our culture today.

In fact, all of these groups taken together still do not seriously threaten justice, mercy, and humble faith. They are merely symptoms of a deeper problem. Even with their access to billions of corporate philanthropy dollars and tax revenues, their huge professional staffs, their monolithic control over the major media outlets, and their stranglehold on the apparatus of cultural power, they do not have the wherewithal to wreak havoc on the essential fabric of our society.

Only one earthly institution has that kind of power: the church.

It is only when the church fails to fulfill its calling in this poor fallen world that we have to really worry. It is only when the church fails to uphold the standards of justice, mercy, and humble faith that the onslaughts of the enemies of truth can possibly have their intended ill-effects. It is only when the church creates a vacuum by its own inactivity and impiety that the minions of this world have the opportunity to exploit the innocent, the foolish, or the inattentive.

That is one of the reasons this book has not been filled with war stories, horror stories, or heart-tugging, tear-jerking, and soul-searching stories. I didn't want to leave the impression that the

ACLU is to blame for the obvious deterioration of justice today, or Planned Parenthood for the absence of mercy, or the NEA for the subversion of humble faith. Because they're not.

The only reason these groups have been able to make headway with their vile plans is that the church has not been all that God has called us to be or done all that God has called us to do. G. K. Chesterton once quipped that any new book of modern social inquiry is bound to be all too predictable in both its form and function:

> It begins as a rule with an analysis, with statistics, with tables of population, decrease of crime among Congregationalists, growth of hysteria among policemen, and similar ascertained facts; it ends with a chapter that is generally called *The Remedy*. It is almost wholly due to this careful, solid, and scientific method that the remedy is never found. For this scheme of medical question and answer is a blunder; the first great blunder of sociology. It is always called stating the disease before we find the cure. But it is the whole definition and dignity of man that in social matters we must actually find the cure before we find the disease.[4]

This book is obviously born of a concern for the disease of moral and social disintegration in our time. But as Chesterton has said, we need not approach our subject medically—which might lead us to trust mere institutional or political remedies. Thus, I have taken the tack of essentially announcing the cure rather than offering yet another diagnosis or description of the malady.

And the cure is simply the church adhering to its essential calling. It is found when the elect of God yield to their divine mandate in every aspect and in every detail of their lives.

A Culture War Maelstrom

One of the greatest men and most brilliant minds Africa ever produced was Augustine of Hippo. He was born in 354 at Tagaste—in present-day Algeria—of a pagan father and a Christian mother. He was brought up as a Christian but not baptized.

He studied rhetoric at the great university in the city of Carthage in order to become a lawyer, but later gave up his plan for a career in teaching. His study of philosophy—with an emphasis on Platonism and Manichaenism—resulted in a complete renunciation of Christianity. He lived a self-confessedly debauched life—including keeping a mistress for fifteen years by whom he had a son.

In pursuit of opportunities to improve his academic standing he took teaching posts—first in Rome and later in Milan. It was in this latter city that he fell under the sway of the great bishop and rhetorician Ambrose. After a long and bitter battle of the soul—described in his classic work *Confessions*—Augustine was converted under Ambrose's ministry and was baptized in 386.

After some two years of intensive discipling and catechizing, he returned to Africa and established a quasi-monastic community in Hippo. There he founded his famous *Classicum Academae*—devoted to study, writing, and the work of cultural transformation. The school was famed for its emphasis on art, music, politics, and ideas.

In 391 Augustine's steadfastness, holiness, and giftedness were recognized, and he was ordained against his own objections. In 394 he was elevated as coadjutor in the diocese. And in 396 he was elevated to the bishopric of the city.

Most of his quite brilliant writings have endured the test of time—I have eight thick volumes that sit on my desk—and are widely read to this day. His commentaries—on Genesis and Psalms particularly—are of inestimable value. His apologetics—like his *Contra Manichae* or *Contra Pelagae*—continue to set the standard for orthodoxy. And his didactae—such as his *Sanctus Dei* or *De Trinitate*—formed the first, and arguably the best, systematic theologies the church has ever produced.

But he is perhaps best known for—and made his greatest contribution with—his analysis of the culture war here on earth and its relation to the war in the heavenlies. Entitled *De Civitate Dei*—or *The City of God*—the book continues to define the terms of the debate better than any other work written before or since.

According to Augustine, culture is not a reflection of a people's race, ethnicity, folklore, politics, language, or heritage. Rather, it is an outworking of a people's creed. In other words, culture is the temporal manifestation of a people's faith. If a culture begins to change, it is not because of fads, fashions, or the passing of time; it is because of a shift in worldview—it is because of a change of faith. Thus, race, ethnicity, folklore, politics, language, or heritage are simply expressions of a deeper paradigm rooted in the covenantal and spiritual matrix of a community's church and the integrity of its witness.

The reason he spent so much of his life and ministry critiquing the pagan philosophies of the world and exposing the aberrant theologies of the church was that Augustine understood only too well that those things matter not only in the realm of eternity determining the spiritual destiny of masses of humanity, but in the realm of the here and now determining the temporal destiny of whole civilizations.

Augustine recognized that people's dominant worldview inevitably shapes the world they have in view. And he also recognized that the church is the starting point for the development of that worldview as it faithfully fulfills its calling to do justice, love mercy, and walk humbly with Almighty God.

Tiny Pushes

Bridging the gap between activism and devotion, the Micah Mandate describes a comprehensive and integrated worldview of vital faith and meaningful activity for the church. It presents what C. S. Lewis called "Mere Christianity," what John Stott called "Basic Christianity," and what William Wilberforce called "Real Christianity."[5] It delineates the ingredients of a balanced Christian life. It provides us with an incentive to walk in the footsteps of those uncommonly common heroes who have gone before us—to get our priorities straight, to put first things first, and to emphasize what really matters most. It outlines a strategic plan for us to begin to do what God wants us to do and to be what God wants us to be.

> It is time for us to change the world with our tiny pushes of justice, mercy, and humble faith.

It offers the church a model not only of fealty and faithfulness but of anticipation and hopefulness as well.

After all, the future of our culture does not depend upon political messiahs or institutional solutions. Neither does it depend on the emergence of some new brilliant spokesman or inspiring leader who has the strength or ability to overcome the forces of darkness.

Instead, the future of our culture depends upon ordinary men and women in the church who are willing to live lives of justice, mercy, and humility before God. It depends on people like you and me who determine to live balanced lives in accord with the good providence of God before a watching world.

Writing to one of her many literary friends, the remarkable blind-deaf-mute, Helen Keller said:

> I long to accomplish a great and noble task, but it is my chief duty to accomplish humble tasks as though they were great and noble. The world is moved along not by the mighty shoves of its heroes, but by the aggregate of the tiny pushes of each honest worker.[6]

Now it is time for all of us who comprise the aggregate to begin to live out the prophetic implications of that kind of faith ourselves by accomplishing the humble tasks of the church's ministry to the world—as though they were great and noble. It is time for us to change the world with our tiny pushes of justice, mercy, and humble faith.

In the end, we must say along with Titus, "These things are excellent and profitable for everyone" (Titus 3:8).

FIGHTING THE GOOD FIGHT

"He has showed you, O man, what is good.
And what does the Lord require of you? To
act justly and to love mercy and to walk
humbly with your God" (Micah 6:8).

It has never been an easy task to keep the church on its proper course. The twin temptations of this poor fallen world—to compromise with the fleshly passions on the one hand and to flee from earthly passions on the other—have always posed great perils to orthodoxy and orthopraxy. Nevertheless, God in His good providence has supplied the church with champions of balanced integrity who have forged for it a great legacy of truth. Examples abound:

Nicholas of Myra (287–340), the fourth-century pastor who inspired the tradition of Santa Claus, may not have lived at the North Pole or traveled by reindeer and sleigh, but he certainly was a paradigm of graciousness, generosity, and Christian charity. His great love and concern for children drew him into a crusade that ultimately resulted in Imperial pro-life statutes that remained in place in Byzantium for more than a thousand years. His tender pastoral care saw his flock through the fierce conflagrations of persecution and heresy. In the end, orthodoxy owed its survival as much to his evident compassion as it did to the theological formulations of his Nicean peers.

Born in Northern Ireland to a wealthy Presbyterian family, *Amy Carmichael* (1867–1951) became one of the best known missionaries of the first half of the twentieth century. Her ministry took her first to Japan, then to Ceylon, and finally to the Dohnavur province of India. Although sarti and immolation had been legally banned, to her horror she discovered that ritual abortion and female infanticide were still quite common. In addition, many of the young girls that she had come to work with were still being systematically sold off as slaves to the nearby pagan temples in order to be raised as cult prostitutes. She immediately established a ministry to protect and shelter the girls. Although she had to suffer the persecution of various Hindu sects and the bureaucratic resistance of the British colonial government, Carmichael built an effective and dynamic ministry renowned for its courage and compassion. Sadly, many of her fellow missionaries in India—having partially accepted the presuppositions of Malthusian thought—believed that her effort to build an orphanage and school was actually a "worldly activity" that distracted her from the "saving of souls." To such accusations she simply replied, "Souls are more or less firmly attached to bodies." Since her death in 1951, her Dohnavur Fellowship has continued to carry on ministries of evangelism, education, and medical aid among the poor and helpless.

Corrie ten Boom (1893–1983) lived with her father and sister in Haarlem, Holland, where she assisted in the family watchmaking business and ministered to a number of mentally retarded children. Early in 1940, the nation fell to the invading Germans. Though at first the occupation seemed bearable enough to Corrie and her family, gradually her Christian conscience was pained as she saw more and more evidence of anti-Semitic persecution. When Jews began to disappear, together the ten Booms began plotting ways to subvert the Nazi's murderous designs. Eventually their home became the hub of the Dutch underground in Haarlem. A secret room was put in one of the bedrooms so that they could hide Jews. In 1944, Corrie was arrested—along with her sister and her father, who both eventually died in German concentration camps—for their illicit rescue efforts. Providentially Corrie was released from prison just a week before her cell block was to be exterminated. For the rest of her life Corrie traveled around the world telling of the consolation and the power of life in Christ. She became a living symbol of the church's persistence of vision.

Dozens of others could be cited throughout the wide span of history: Cyprian of Carthage (d. 258), Antony of Egypt (d. 356), Hilary of Poitiers (d. 367), Bede (d. 735), Alcuin (d. 804), John Owen (d. 1683), and Oswald Chambers (d. 1917). Each demonstrated the reality that the church is a perpetually defeated thing that always survives its conquerors—as long as it remains faithful to its call to do justice, love mercy, and walk humbly with Almighty God.

AGAINST ALL ODDS

"He has showed you, O man, what is good.
And what does the Lord require of you? To act
justly and to love mercy and to walk humbly
with your God" (Micah 6:8).

Review the "impossible" situations of the Bible:
from the stories of Abraham, Moses, David, and
Elijah to the predicaments of Gideon, Daniel,
Lazarus, and Paul. Then reread the paeon to faith in
Hebrews 11–12. When we walk by faith and not by
sight, the odds look significantly better, don't they?

Make a list of all the "impossible" situations the
church faces in our own day: from cultural disarray
and social disintegration to legalized abortion and a
biased media. Begin to pray specifically that God
would raise up new champions in each of these
areas to confound the rebellious in the world and
the recalcitrant in the church.

Now, make a list of all the "impossible" situations in
your own life. Select a passage of Scripture to
memorize that outlines some aspect of God's "very
great and precious promises" (2 Peter 1:4) relating
to each.

Finally, go to work. Face the odds. Do what God
has called you to do. Be what God has called you to
be. And always remember: The church is "Plan A" in
God's great scheme of things—and there is no
"Plan B."

Notes

1. George Grant, *Trial and Error: The American Civil Liberties Union and Its Impact on Your Family* (Franklin, Tenn.: Adroit Press, 1993).

2. George Grant, *Grand Illusions: The Legacy of Planned Parenthood* (Franklin, Tenn.: Adroit Press, 1992).

3. George Grant, *The Family Under Siege: What the New Social Engineers Have in Mind for You and Your Children* (Minneapolis: Bethany, 1994).

4. G. K. Chesterton, *What's Wrong with the World* (New York: Dodd Mead, 1910), 1.

5. C. S. Lewis, *Mere Christianity* (New York: Macmillan, 1952); John Stott, *Basic Christianity* (Downers Grove, Ill.: InterVarsity, 1971); William Wilberforce, *Real Christianity* (Portland, Ore.: Multnomah, 1982).

6. H. Lyndon Kilmer, *Helen Keller* (New York: Skillen & Fortas, 1964), 164.